Darrell
Knowlton

PARTNERS IN CHANGE

"*Right on target . . .*"

"This reference manual really hit home. The author has covered all areas of AA, NA, and . . . Twelve Step programs for family members. [*Partners in Change* is] an excellent tool to aid officers in counseling the chemically dependent offender—one of the best [books] I have read on what is actually occurring in community-based corrections. I believe state credentialing boards should recommend this book to every professional seeking certification. [It's] a must for all persons in the field of corrections, law enforcement, treatment providers, and social services."

—JAMES E. DARE
Director of Adult Probation
Montgomery County, Ohio, Court of Common Pleas

"*This is very good work . . .*"

"The author has addressed almost every issue imaginable on this subject. The book is very practical; it is very much on target. . . . I found the glossary of program vernacular to be extremely helpful. Also helpful to the correctional employee will be the section 'Working with Resistance.' This book does an excellent job of providing a historical overview of Alcoholics Anonymous."

—ROBERT HARRISON
Correctional Manager III
Former Parole Services Administrator for the State of Kansas

"The text has an easy, conversational tone, and an element of passion comes through every page. The work's main message is that the task of facilitating offender recovery is not futile. We have to value what we are 'selling,' and treat each offender as an individual. Understanding and knowledge of addiction and the Twelve Step recovery process are key."

—DENNIS AVERY
Manager of Adult Field Services
Hennepin County, Minnesota, Community Corrections

PARTNERS IN CHANGE

The Twelve Step Referral Handbook
for Probation, Parole, and Community Corrections

Edward M. Read, LCSW, NCAC II

U.S. Probation Officer for the U.S. District Court

District of Columbia

Hazelden
Center City, Minnesota 55012-0176

American Correctional Association
4380 Forbes Boulevard
Lanham, Maryland 20706-4322

ISBN: 1-56838-101-8

Editor's note

Hazelden offers a variety of information on chemical dependency and related areas. Our publications do not necessarily represent Hazelden's programs, nor do they officially speak for any Twelve Step organization.

The American Correctional Association offers a variety of information for those in the correctional field. Readers are encouraged to call (1-800-ACA-Join) for a free, complete catalogue of publications.

The Twelve Steps of Alcoholics Anonymous and Twelve Traditions of Alcoholics Anonymous are reprinted with permission of Alcoholics Anonymous World Services, Inc. Permission to reprint this material does not mean that AA has reviewed or approved the content of this publication nor that AA agrees with the views expressed herein. AA is a program of recovery from alcoholism. Use of the Twelve Steps and Twelve Traditions in connection with programs that are patterned after AA but which address other problems does not imply otherwise.

To my darling daughter, *Sofia;* my loving wife, *Lee;* and in memory of my dear mother, *Henrietta;* three strong and inspirational females who together, one in infancy, one in marriage, and one in death, represent and give ultimate meaning to my life today.

Contents

DEDICATION V

PREFACE XI

CHAPTER 1. THE CHALLENGE: COMMUNITY SUPERVISION OF THE ADDICTED
          OFFENDER 1

        Introduction 1
        The Addiction Problem: A Multidimensional Perspective 2
        On Becoming Part of the Solution 5
        It Works If You Work It 5
        Toward Twelve Step Literacy: A New Objective 7
        How to Use This Book 8

CHAPTER 2. GETTING STRAIGHT: ON ATTITUDES, FACTS, AND ACTION 11

        Drugs *and* Attitudes Kill 11
        The Power of Selective Recall 12
        H.O.W. to Take OUR Inventory 13
        The Other Offender: Self-Righteous Indignation (SRI) 15
        Fiction on Addiction: SRI Thinking Scenarios 16
        Dual Disorders: Addiction Gets a Bum Rap 26
        A Conspiracy of Silence: On Alcohol 28
        Disease versus Willful Misconduct 32
        Out of the C.A.G.E. and into Assessment 35
        Into Action: "Raising the Bottom" with Positive Authority 38

CHAPTER 3. FIRST THINGS FIRST: UNDERSTANDING HISTORY THROUGH
        TRADITION 41

    In Retrospect: From Then to Now 41

    "Upside Down" Anarchy: Understanding the Traditions 44

    Protecting the Fellowship: In Twelve Ways 46

        The First Tradition: Unity versus Individualism 46

        The Second Tradition: Who's in Charge? 47

        The Third Tradition: Who Can Attend? 47

        The Fourth Tradition: Autonomy with a Caveat 49

        The Fifth Tradition: No Hidden Agendas 49

        The Sixth Tradition: No Endorsements 50

        The Seventh Tradition: No Dues, Only Expenses 50

        The Eighth Tradition: AA is Nonprofessional 51

        The Ninth Tradition: Organized Freedom 52

        The Tenth Tradition: None of Our Business 53

        The Eleventh Tradition: Attraction versus Promotion 53

        The Twelfth Tradition: Principles before Personalities 54

    Narcotics Anonymous Comes of Age: A Brief History 55

    Correcting Misconceptions: A Quick Review 57

CHAPTER 4. STEP BY STEP: AN INSIDE VIEW OF THE TWELVE STEPS 61

    Introduction 61

    The Foundation Steps (1–3) 63

        Step One: Or, I Can't Stop Alone 63

        Step Two: Or, We Can Stop Together 64

        Step Three: Or, Making a Commitment to the Program 65

    Steps of Reflection (4–6) 67

        Step Four: Or, Taking an Honest Look at Myself 67

        Step Five: Or, Sharing the Human Connection 69

        Step Six: Or, Getting Ready to Move on in Sobriety 71

    Steps of Reconciliation (7–9) 72

        Step Seven: Or, Asking for Help Again 72

        Step Eight: Or, Identifying the Victims 73

        Step Nine: Or, Into Action on the Amends 74

    The Maintenance Steps (10–12) 75

        Step Ten: Or, Self-Examination While "Clean" 75

        Step Eleven: Or, Learning to Grow through Meditation 76

        Step Twelve: Or, Beginning to Help Others 78

CHAPTER 5. WORKING THE PROGRAM: PRACTICAL SUPERVISION TECHNIQUES 81

The Hidden Message 81
Doing *Our* Homework 82
Types of Meetings 83
Shaping the Referral: A Proactive Model 89
   Refer; ReRefer; and Re-Re-Refer 89
   Referral Objectives 90
   "Standard Referrals" 91
Other "Referral Packages" 95
NA versus AA: Some Observations 95
Program Options for Nonbelievers 97
Working *with* Resistance 99
Slip-Signing Scams 108
Sponsorship: Use It or Lose It! 112
Professional Parameters on Sponsorship 118
Wrapping It Up with "Do's and Don'ts" 120

CHAPTER 6. COMPANION COMMUNITY RESOURCES 125

Introduction 125
The Addicted Family System 126
Al-Anon: Common Misconceptions 132
What Al-Anon Is and Is Not 133
The Newcomer Asks 134
Al-Anon "Works" the Twelve Steps 137
Nar-Anon Family Groups: Still Growing 139
Community Supervision Techniques 140
Notes on Postresidential Treatment 142
On Going Home: Prescription for Relapse? 143
Oxford House: A Workable "Geographic Cure" 144
Summary 148

CHAPTER 7. A COLLECTIVE RESPONSE: SUPERVISION ACCOUNTABILITY
   REVISITED 149

Responding to the Challenge 149
"Systemic Recovery": An Analogy 150
Final Thoughts: Toward a New Paradigm 152

APPENDIX A: A COMPENDIUM OF MUTUAL SUPPORT GROUPS 155

APPENDIX B: SUGGESTED READING 171

"WALKING THE TALK": A GLOSSARY OF "PROGRAM" VERNACULAR 173

INDEX 181

ABOUT THE AUTHOR 185

Preface

This is written as a "handbook" and thus is not necessarily meant for cover-to-cover reading. It *is* meant to have on your desk, ready and available for consultation. It contains resource information, referral tips, and practical notes about the Twelve Step programs vis-à-vis probation, parole, and all of community corrections.

In my capacity as a line federal probation officer committed to working with the addicted offender, I have certain professional biases and convictions about my work that have seeped through the pages. I make no apologies for this; simply be mindful of this as you read. For example, any and all references to the Twelve Step fellowships are in no way an official representation of their membership or headquarters. Similarly, absent a specifically cited source, what is written will be the author's opinion and/or experience.

There are other housekeeping matters that require attention. References to Alcoholics Anonymous (AA) or any of the other Twelve Step programs should be presumed to extend to all such programs, unless specifically stated otherwise. Words or phrases such as *alcoholic, drug-dependent, substance abuser, addict,* and *user* have been used interchangeably throughout. Since the term *offender* has been officially adopted by the Federal Probation System, we will mostly use it despite the knowledge that many still prefer *client.*

Finally, a word of thanks and acknowledgment to my wife, Lee Trevino, also a Federal Probation Officer within a neighboring jurisdiction, for the time she devoted to proofing and editing this manuscript. Thanks to Rus Harbaugh, for his special friendship throughout the past ten years and without whom I could not have completed this project.

Chapter 1

The Challenge:
Community Supervision of the Addicted Offender

Introduction

Try as we might, we cannot cure addiction, no matter what the money, politics, or collective resolve. Substance abuse is here to stay and by current scientific standards is still incurable. This may change over time, we can all hope, as research and development continue, but today we must satisfy ourselves with prevention, control, education, and treatment. Substance abuse is a major national problem; some might argue it is a national public health emergency.

It is estimated there are currently at least five million drug abusers and eighteen million or more alcohol abusers in need of treatment.[1] One out of four Americans experiences family problems related to alcohol abuse. Economically, substance abuse consumes over $238 billion annually, including costs for unnecessary health care, extra law enforcement, automobile accidents, crime, and lost productivity. Sadly, only about one-fourth of those needing substance abuse treatment ever actually receive it. The bottom line is not at all attractive: each year nearly one-half million American people die from alcohol, tobacco, and illicit drugs, making substance abuse without a doubt our country's single largest preventable cause of death.

As most of our readers well know, the criminal justice system by default has become a key player in the midst of this crisis, taking on perhaps more than its fair share of the overall social, economic, and political fallout. More than three million arrests are made each year for alcohol-related offenses alone. At least one-half of all people arrested for major crimes such as homicide, theft, and assault

---

1. Unless otherwise indicated, these statistics are from *Substance Abuse: The Nation's Number One Health Problem (Key Indicators for Policy)*, prepared by Institute for Health Policy, Brandeis University, for The Robert Wood Johnson Fd., Princeton, N.J., 1993.

were under the influence of illicit drugs at the time of their arrest. Imagine what the reports might reveal had these numbers included alcohol as a drug of abuse and/or had they counted minor offenses.

Most drug or alcohol abusers do not commit crimes. However, most criminals do abuse alcohol and drugs. It is estimated that as many as 70 percent of all offenders have serious problems with alcohol and other drugs, and that their use has in some way caused or exacerbated their legal predicament.[2] According to the National Institute of Justice, anywhere from 53 to 82 percent of male arrestees in a variety of urban areas tested positive for at least one drug, not including alcohol.[3] Addiction is clearly and disproportionately overrepresented within the criminal offender population.

The Addiction Problem: A Multidimensional Perspective

For the purposes of this book we are defining community corrections professionals as probation, parole, and all other personnel responsible for either direct-supervision accountability or correctional treatment of addicted offenders within the community, including contract drug treatment, pre-release, and other alternative programming staff. Although we have written largely from the probation officer's perspective, the information this book offers is extremely valuable to others within the court family, the community corrections system, or even institutional settings, including criminal lawyers, judges, prison counselors, and halfway house workers.

The primary mission statement of the community corrections system is this: *To carry out specific court or paroling authority mandates by modifying or changing offender behavior through strategic behavioral intervention so that we may protect and maintain public safety.* Most court jurisdictions, including county, state, and federal probation offices, will generally mirror something close to this type of overall policy directive. To fulfill this mission we must identify the behavior of the offender in need of attention. As outlined above, well over half and perhaps as many as two-thirds of the offenders under our various jurisdictions are in trouble with drugs, alcohol, or, more likely, a combination of both. Thus the first and most obvious issue to address is the addiction problem: its sheer pervasiveness and depth. It is inescapable.

2. Terence T. Gorski, *Relapse Prevention Therapy with Chemically Dependent Criminal Offenders: A Guide for Counselors, Therapists, and Criminal Justice Professionals* (Independence, Mo.: Herald House, 1994), 17.
3. Marie Ragghianti and Toni Glenn, *Reducing Recidivism: Treating the Addicted Inmate* (Center City, Minn.: Hazelden, 1991), 1.

Yet despite the pervasiveness of the problem, the criminal justice system, generally, does not hire staff with specialized training in the field of chemical dependency or addictions. Typically, the organizational assumption is that since the persons were qualified to be probation officers (or counselors, or caseworkers) in the first place and, therefore, must have a working knowledge of human behavior, then logically their field of vision and counseling skills could extend to substance abuse. Most of us know that this is not the case. Supplemental and even specialized training in this area is critical to the performance of our mission. Additionally, we are not all cut from the same mold. Some of us work better with addicts and alcoholics than others. And all of us should at least have the opportunity to improve our professional knowledge base and maximize our effectiveness with whatever population we feel most comfortable.

Ironically, though we may not understand the nature of substance abuse ourselves, we still demand serious change of our addicted offenders. We insist that they come to accept the existence of their problem; that they motivate themselves to learn and pursue new knowledge about their addiction; and that they initiate attitudinal and behavioral changes designed to sustain their new understanding of themselves and their condition. If we expect them to understand and get a handle on their addiction, we cannot continue the "Do as I say and not as I do" paradigm. We must reach beyond issuing orders and become truly knowledgeable about our subject matter if we want to effect behavioral change.

The reality, of course, is that the money to carry out this new organizational resolve will not always be there, if in fact it ever was. The nation's current political sound bites emphasize the need to find ways of "doing more with less." Although the probation system is destined for rising caseloads of substance-abusing offenders, expanding community programs, alternative sentencing, and a growing reluctance to continue "warehousing" nonviolent first-time drug users, the economic reality will not extend much beyond limited allocation for new staff. Money is not likely to pour into training coffers; nor will we feel much direct impact from the government's interest in refocusing on demand reduction or prevention and treatment efforts. This means that we must be creative. We must access and pool available resources within the community.

Recovery from addiction demands a personal commitment to end the isolation, to stop the destructive cycle of obsessive self-reliance, and to reach out for help. Similarly, we will be challenged to put to rest our own fantasies about the impact we can singularly or individually have on the addicted offender. Alone, we are simply not that powerful. The addiction problem is much bigger than our individual counseling skills or experience. We must move out from behind our desks and into the recovering community as we search for resourceful and experienced allies.

Criminal justice professionals, taken as a group, are not generally known for their singleness of purpose or method. To be sure, we all try various ways to "correct" deviant behavior, "rehabilitate" offenders, and provide structured supervision for them. All this very sincere effort is, of course, in the name of an overriding mandate calling for public safety. Unfortunately, our purpose diminishes in view of dramatic methodological differences. We have divergent strategies, unique interactional styles, and fundamental philosophical differences. This situation becomes even more pronounced as we look for ways to combat alcohol and other drug addictions within the community. The addiction problem becomes a feeding ground for differences of opinion.

For example, one court jurisdiction will profess "zero tolerance" for illicit drug use of any kind, even once. The "disease concept" of addiction is without meaning to them. And yet another office may work within the context of the disease model and be far slower to react adversely. Many of us are far too lenient, in fact. We become enablers or simply lose interest and burn out. Others end up passing moralistic judgment.

Alcohol elicits similar controversy. It is acknowledged as a powerfully addictive chemical (or drug) by some. Yet, for others, it remains shrouded in a dangerous conspiracy of silence or unconscious denial system.

We are in a perpetual state of conflict when it comes to our offenders and their addictions. We disagree about nearly everything, including etiology (how the addiction got started in the first place), treatment styles, and responsibility issues. The harsh reality is that the "experts" are still hard at work to develop answers to the tough questions about addiction.

The addiction problem *is* alarmingly complex and multidimensional. Hundreds of studies and hundreds of thousands of dollars later, the single most important finding about the cause of addiction is this: "The etiology of drug dependence is complex and multifactorial, depending on the interplay of many factors."[4] No wonder chemical dependency treatment remains a mysterious and challenging quest!

---

4. A. Arif and J. Westermeyer. *Manual of Drug and Alcohol Abuse* (New York: Plenum Publishing, 1988), 81.

On Becoming Part of the Solution

The good news is that many offenders *do* recover, get better, turn themselves around, and remain out of trouble for extended periods of time. For some the turning point arrives spontaneously, devoid of obvious precipitators. Something happens to them. Something changes them. Perhaps the third parole revocation makes that elusive "connection" for the addict. Maybe it is nothing more than growing older and losing energy or enthusiasm for the hustle.

The problem is that, as it stands now, we cannot precisely *predict* what will happen to offenders. This is the crux of our challenge as we work with this population. We are dealing with an inexact science. We are working with human beings, all unique in their makeup and constitution.

If our primary purpose as it relates to working with addicted offenders is to get them clean and sober, then it should be our professional obligation to our chemically dependent offenders to refer them to the experts: Alcoholics Anonymous (AA), Narcotics Anonymous (NA), and other Twelve Step programs. The recovering alcoholic opens an AA meeting by reciting something like the following: "Our primary purpose is to stay sober and help other alcoholics to achieve sobriety." This singleness of purpose has yielded phenomenal success throughout the world for sixty years now: millions of recovering persons can testify to this reality.

The complexities of alcohol and drug addiction treatment go beyond even the most seasoned professional's individual counseling skills. Therefore, we must seek out the help of successfully recovering people within our communities, the ones we know exist and are doing well. They are the real experts.

It Works If You Work It

Why refer every addict or alcoholic? It is almost so simple we forget. We do it because we want to capitalize on what we know is successful, on what we know works out there beyond our office doors. Let us put aside the etiological or philosophical debates, at least until we master the single aspect of chemical dependency treatment upon which virtually all of us agree. After all, it is the central theme that repeatedly makes its appearance within the lives of recovering addicts and alcoholics: for all but a very small minority, active involvement in a Twelve Step program or self-help group plays a critical role in long-term or sustained abstinence. There is no debate about this.

Reflect on the history of your caseloads, especially consider those that made it. How many of the addicted offenders had at least one foot in the door of AA,

NA, or some other Twelve Step group? Conversely, as you reflect on the failures, how many of them resisted involvement in the groups? Notice any correlation? Offenders who have a foundation in the Fellowship and actually try to work their program have a much better chance of staying out of court and jail. Sadly, the system does not take the time or spend the money for controlled research. Those of us who have worked in the field of addictions know the truth: As they say in the meetings, "It works if you work it."

Since the development of AA in the 1930s, thought by many to be one of the most important social phenomena of the twentieth century, myriad other Twelve Step programs have formed and fashioned themselves after it. For the sake of simplicity, we will use Alcoholics Anonymous as the general centerpiece for this book. The Twelve Steps of AA are the same Twelve Steps used for Narcotics Anonymous (NA), Overeaters Anonymous (OA), Gamblers Anonymous (GA), or Sex and Love Addicts Anonymous (SLAA). Here are the Steps in full; we will discuss them separately, later.

The Twelve Steps of Alcoholics Anonymous[5]

1. We admitted we were powerless over alcohol—that our lives had become unmanageable.

2. Came to believe that a Power greater than ourselves could restore us to sanity.

3. Made a decision to turn our will and our lives over to the care of God *as we understood Him.*

4. Made a searching and fearless moral inventory of ourselves.

5. Admitted to God, to ourselves, and to another human being the exact nature of our wrongs.

6. Were entirely ready to have God remove all these defects of character.

7. Humbly asked Him to remove our shortcomings.

8. Made a list of all persons we had harmed, and became willing to make amends to them all.

---

5. The Twelve Steps of Alcoholics Anonymous are taken from *Alcoholics Anonymous,* 3d ed., published by Alcoholics Anonymous World Services, Inc., New York, N.Y., 59–60. Reprinted with permission. (See editor's note on copyright page.)

9. Made direct amends to such people wherever possible, except when to do so would injure them or others.

10. Continued to take personal inventory and when we were wrong promptly admitted it.

11. Sought through prayer and meditation to improve our conscious contact with God *as we understood Him,* praying only for the knowledge of His will for us and the power to carry that out.

12. Having had a spiritual awakening as the result of these steps, we tried to carry this message to alcoholics, and to practice these principles in all our affairs.

Note: The Steps for Narcotics Anonymous (NA) are almost identical. Simply substitute the word *addiction* for *alcohol* in Step One and *addicts* for *alcoholics* in Step Twelve, and place the word *We* at the beginning of Steps Two through Twelve.

Walk into any nationally recognized residential treatment center and ask about the emphasis placed on Twelve Step programs modeled after AA. Talk to the "addictionologists," employee assistance professionals, and front-line counselors about what they consider essential to recovery. (Invariably, they will mention the Twelve Steps.) We need not personally experience drug abuse, become recovering addicts ourselves, or return to graduate school to achieve results with this population, but we do require command of the Twelve Step program.

Toward Twelve Step Literacy: A New Objective

Simply directing a client to attend AA once a week is not enough. For many offenders, we will be the ones responsible for their very first introduction to the Twelve Step process. Most will be in some phase of denial. Many will be manipulative and resistant to the prospects of mandatory attendance. Really knowing the program, feeling comfortable with the Steps, and being able to discuss them intelligently begin to assume critical significance.

Yes, many of us are already routinely referring appropriate offenders to Twelve Step groups in the community. That, in fact, may be part of the problem in the first place: the perfunctory AA referral. A satisfactory referral to a Twelve Step program cannot be perfunctory. How informed are we? How much conviction do we have that it really can work? Do we communicate cynicism? Do we have the resolve to stick with it and work with or through the resistance? How literate are we in discussing someone's program involvement without benefit of court slips?

Our purpose in writing this book is twofold: First, and at the expense of that all too fleeting commodity called humility, we hope to change an attitude, even ever so slightly, about the nature of addiction and how community corrections should work with drug and alcohol offenders. Attitude change must precede action. We cannot simultaneously look down our noses at the alcoholic or other addict and hope to initiate positive change. It will not happen, not with this population. They are far too sensitive and intelligent to respond under such conditions, unless they do so possibly out of spite. And that happens only rarely.

The second objective, and perhaps the medium through which the first will be sought, is to move toward Twelve Step literacy: to educate the community corrections system about the use of, cooperation with, and significance of Twelve Step groups in general, and the fellowships of AA and NA, in particular, as they relate to community supervision of the addicted adult offender. There are a variety of opinions and feelings about these groups. The goal will be to clear the air and put an end to the confusion and misinformation about our referral techniques.

How to Use This Book

This book is not meant to be read cover to cover. It certainly can be and we would not discourage it. Realistically, we do not expect it. We are overworked! Caseloads are much too high; the paperwork and administrative demands are daunting. There is no surplus of time, either in the field or the office. Unless involved in specialized chemical dependency caseloads or experimental programs, we rarely have the time to extend ourselves to the community and visit Twelve Step meetings firsthand, whether it be on our own time, while working in the field, or otherwise. There will not be time to implement many of the practical suggestions contained in this resource guide. We recognize these constraints and have tried to put the book together in a way that will maximize its usefulness to the reader.

If nothing else, read chapters 4 and 5. These two chapters form the heart and soul of our message. Again, understanding the Twelve Steps and learning the techniques necessary to make appropriate referrals is our professional responsibility. We have done our best to provide more than just the basics. Keep in mind that all of our chapters stand alone comfortably. Expect occasional repetition, because reading this book does not depend on reading the chapters in order. It is designed to be referred to, looked over when needed, and kept on the desk next to the dictionary and other reference material. See what can be used and disregard that which is not helpful until the time or need arises, depending on the particular needs of the offender. Or, as they say in AA, take what you need and leave the rest. Remember: we cannot handle this difficult population alone. As we emphasize throughout, it takes a collective effort. Consider making this book a part of the team!

CHAPTER 2

Getting Straight:
On Attitudes, Facts, and Action

Drugs *and* Attitudes Kill

No argument about the drugs. And yes, bad attitudes also kill these days. Sometimes it is quick and tragic and other times it occurs much more slowly. Whether it be a teenager's ill-advised posturing on the street corner ("You dissed me, man") or a veteran probation officer's bad attitude about his addicted offender ("I got a real problem working those substance-abuse cases"), in either instance, with but a slight stretch of the imagination, unintentional loss may be the end result. One is an error of commission; the other, perhaps, of omission. An illegally purchased semiautomatic pistol might hasten the end of a life in the first instance. In the other, a probation officer's attitude, steeped in no less potentially danger-ous anger, ignorance, or prejudice, may work passively but painstakingly behind the scenes to either damage the relationship between officer and offender or cause the officer to look the other way when he or she should not have. Once the dam-age becomes irreparable and the relationship is lost, there is very little opportunity for the seeds of recovery to "take."

Working with addicted offenders is virtually unavoidable today, regardless of how specialized an office may be administratively. Even for the seasoned criminal justice professional, addicted offenders are a formidable challenge. Unfortunately, the stereotypical adjectives used to describe this population during their active addiction often do fit: words like *manipulative, dishonest, antagonistic, antisocial, narcissistic,* and *deceitful.*

So, once again, the challenge awaits us to push beyond these negative symptoms and inch the offender forward, toward the goals of abstinence, personality change, and a positive way of life. This is early recovery; it is very much externally moti-vated at first. To witness an offender turn around, get with the program, stay clean and sober for a period of time, and make the shift to self-motivation is surely a high point for many of us.

The Power of Selective Recall

There are very real personal and professional rewards to working with the addicted offender population. Many of us have learned to consciously and selectively recall the good cases—remembering them, talking about them, and rekindling the reality that some offenders do make it. It is important that we hang on to the memory of those cases and share in their remarkable personal revolutions (recovery is about total change). Typically, these are the special individuals who overcome tremendous odds as they learn to cold-shoulder their old ways of life and accept their new direction and fellowship in the program. By keeping their stories fresh in our minds, much as the alcoholic or addict must keep the memory and pain of addiction alive to stay sober, we get through the rough-and-tumble, more cynical days of outrageous caseloads, administrative responsibilities, and paperwork.

There is another part of our work with this population that warrants comment. For many of us, the addicted offenders are easier to understand and relate to than many of the other classic or nonaddicted offenders whose criminal behavior and lifestyle often seem so morally repugnant. This is because for many drug offenders (though by no means all), there is a context, cultural or otherwise, within which to understand the addict's underlying offense or prior pattern of offenses. This does not explain away or depreciate the seriousness of the original crime; it simply provides helpful background information and suggests that if the individuals can get beyond the denial, accept their condition, and become abstinent, there is a chance that they will not commit additional offenses. Criminal behavior, in many of these cases, is largely symptomatic of the primary problem: addiction. Thus, failure to make a distinction between addicted and nonaddicted offenders—essentially adopting the attitude that "a criminal is a criminal is a criminal"—will inevitably cause us to miss numerous opportunities to help guide and effect true rehabilitation.

But what about the "good" cases, the ones that do respond to intervention or somehow spontaneously "get it"? What happens with them? Why does the light bulb suddenly go on? Sometimes not even the offenders can tell us. There is one thing we do know—this person undergoes a profound attitude change that begins with acceptance: "I accept the indisputable fact that I am in big trouble *because of* booze and dope!" There is a clear connection and logic to the thought process.

The shift is made from a state of complete denial to one of total acceptance. Getting the offender to this point is one of our greatest challenges. How do we help the addicted offender make this otherwise elusive cognitive connection between getting high and doing time? We help by taking action ourselves.

H.O.W. to Take OUR Inventory

Clever acronyms and short slogans have always been a trademark of the Twelve Step group vernacular. Though these slogans and acronyms may seem painfully trite early on, newcomers nonetheless often latch on to favorites, the ones that best describe their particular stumbling blocks to sobriety. People who have been around a few years find added practicality in many of them as they put them to use in other aspects of their day-to-day life. The slogans have a special efficacy for people who are in varying states of crisis, need structured reassurance, or tend to complicate matters. In fact, many program members say half-jokingly that their meetings are for "simple people who like to complicate things." One thing is for certain: the most popularized slogan, seen on bumper stickers and elsewhere, is "Keep it simple."

In the spirit of keeping it simple, here is the point: *Many of these slogans, if used, would do wonders for the community corrections system!* They work well for anyone trying to live life on life's terms or anyone interested in approaching his or her work with equanimity and quiet resolve. Consequently, we will make an effort to weave as many of them as possible throughout this book to demonstrate their practicality for both the criminal justice professional and the addict or alcoholic.

H.O.W. the program works or H.O.W. an individual gets clean and sober are fundamental questions posed by both insiders and outsiders. There is a short and a long answer. The short answer is more than captured by the acronym itself. It refers to the wisdom contained in the words *H*onesty, *O*pen-mindedness, and *W*illingness. These words are truly incisive, as they cut to the core of the program, its principles, and what it takes for an individual addict or alcoholic to get straight. Now for the long answer.

*H*onesty. Imagine having first to confront, at gut level, the humiliating reality of being powerless over an addiction, the very thing that for these people makes life worthwhile or livable. This is the first layer of honesty, perhaps the most important, too; for it squares off with and eventually overtakes denial. The honesty gets deeper as the layers of the onion are peeled away; addicts get to know themselves better and better the longer they stop running from themselves. One moves from "cash-register" honesty to levels of honesty involving relationships, self ("to thine own self be true"), and spirituality.

*O*pen-mindedness. It allows addicts to begin the acceptance process and to see that there may be a way out; that perhaps if they listen and open themselves up to others, there will be a payoff. Maybe if they consider following directions (from a sponsor, for example) and relaxing their own selfish and typically myopic standards, they might find themselves putting some clean time together.

*W*illingness. If it were possible to do an autopsy on the spirit of someone's long-term recovery, someone whose abstemious lifestyle had been characterized by comfortable, peaceful, and selfless devotion to others, the concept of willingness would appear pervasive. Absent some degree of willingness, there will be no change in the first place. There will not even be movement in the right direction of change. Without change there certainly will be no meaningful recovery. Am I willing to be honest? Am I willing to be open-minded? Am I willing to pray for the willingness to be willing?

The bottom line for us in community corrections is no different from that of the actively addicted offender: Before we can "monitor" and "supervise" someone's recovery process (or lack thereof), we must first accept the need for our own change of attitude. We must start at home, by taking a good hard look at ourselves, from the inside out. We must implement the H.O.W. of the program by looking within and taking a personal inventory of where we stand against the challenge of working with addicted offenders in the community.

How *H*onest are we about what we really know about addiction? How *O*pen-minded are we to new information? How *W*illing are we to change or at least significantly restructure our attitudes about addiction in general? With the reality of not having all the answers, how willing are we to stumble forward, toward an attitude grounded in personal accountability, responsibility to the truth, and reasonable compassion for the victim of a potentially fatal disease?

We are intelligent and experienced professionals who are, for the most part, completely devoted to the fulfillment of our community, court, or parole mandates. Of course, we are not perfect. We are bright enough that our subtle shades of prejudice often masquerade as legitimate opinion or sanctimonious theory, absent any scientific foundation. This can be very dangerous to all of us, not just the addicted offender. Can we challenge ourselves to move beyond this, to identify the bad attitudes for what they are and work toward a positive and open-minded change of perspective?

Our professional mandate calls for us to assist in the protection of society by supervising persons in the community who have undergone court or paroling authority directives consequent to criminal behavior. We cannot satisfy these conditions, or this mandate, by paperwork alone. Much as it would seem to the contrary, in terms of inadequate funding and the toll it takes on our caseloads, it is impossible to do our job without bumping into a warm body. The overwhelming majority of these bodies will be in trouble with alcohol or drugs. We must see them, talk to them, and relate to them. And yes, we must try to form relationships—sometimes on the fly—but try we must! The better the relationship, the more information available, and, ultimately, the more accountability to our mission. By setting the stage for mutual respect, both for the offender as a person and for the addictive disease, we minimize the negative effects of our greatest detractor, the "other offender."

The Other Offender: Self-Righteous Indignation (SRI)

Let's face it. We know that when it comes to the addicted offender, a complete change of attitude from one of killer denial to full acceptance of one's addictive disease will make all the difference in the world. We also know that some of us are better than others at changing our own attitudes. Some of us prefer to hold on to bad attitudes or thinking habits, often much longer than reasonably warranted. We covet them. They are familiar. And over time they become dangerously transfixed as part of our "worldview."

This other offender, disguised as an attitude formation, seeps in when we least expect it, often barely noticeable at first. Unfortunately, it confuses the supervision process and circumvents any effort to effectively intervene with someone's drug or alcohol addiction. We admonish the reader to know the enemy! Get familiar with your detractors. This is good advice for a businessperson as well as a community corrections professional.

We have labeled and defined this package of prejudicial attitudes, feelings, and raw opinion about addiction as *self-righteous indignation*.

SELF-RIGHTEOUS INDIGNATION

A narrow-minded, patronizing, or moralistic attitude toward different lifestyles, often laced with free-floating anger.

There is nothing wrong with morality per se. Definitely not. As criminal justice workers, we must teach and exhibit behavior that distinguishes right from wrong as a part of our job. Even becoming indignant or angry about certain behaviors is not necessarily objectionable, provided it serves a counseling or therapeutic purpose. What is damaging to the supervision process is what happens when narrow-minded morality, particularly as it relates to lifestyles, is coupled with anger. It is not a good mix. Mutual respect for one another (officer/counselor to offender), *as human beings,* is not possible in the midst of such patronization. As a consequence, our dual interest in community protection and individual accountability or change will never become a reality.

This is not meant to indict the entire profession. Few of us are driven by this type of rigid attitude formation, but with the swing between the law enforcement and social work aspects of the supervision process, there is plenty of room for needless faltering.

Why is the anger part of SRI so prevalent in the first place? Probably for many different reasons—all very personal, subjective, and difficult to pinpoint rationally. For some it may be one's own family experience with substance abuse, typically alcoholism. Or perhaps it has to do with having trouble maintaining our own interpersonal boundaries. Some people are more compassionate than others and have the ability to see without the blinders, to recognize differences in culture, experience, and values. Many of us unconsciously find ourselves in the corrections field, replete with opportunities to control others, for the wrong reasons. Some of us need to control and repeatedly exercise authority over others as a means of assuaging our own insecurity.

For the majority, the problem is much simpler: lack of education about addiction. If you don't know about it, have not been exposed to it, and are not challenged by or seeking new information—in this case about addictive disease and the recovery process—the result will be fertile ground for various shades of the SRI attitude base.

Self-righteous indignation exists to some extent within each and every one of us. None of us can completely escape its vestiges, no matter how enlightened we may feel about our work with addicts and alcoholics. Therefore, it is up to each of us as individuals to work to stay vigilant.

Fiction on Addiction: SRI Thinking Scenarios

To get the introspective wheels turning, here are some thinking scenarios that typify the various shades of SRI, as previously defined, and show how dangerous such a mixture of attitudes and feelings about addiction can be. They are fiction-alized to make a point. Sadly, the general ideas they reflect are not fiction. However, they are purposely exaggerated and stereotyped to serve as an educational tool. The scenarios all begin with one seemingly harmless word, which in a community corrections context establishes a negative tone from the beginning. The word is *those*. Right away it negates individuality and sets a patronizing tone.

BAD CHOICES BY BAD PEOPLE
(or, the Power of Cultural Context?)

Those addicts are all pretty stupid, if you ask me. I don't get it. Why even try something like crack cocaine or heroin? I mean even once! It's so stupid. Look at the media hype, the educational onslaught, and the mandatory minimums. Come on . . . and they still decide to hit the pipe or find a vein! Something's wrong with them. I'm sorry, it makes no sense at all. It's so obvious. Those people don't reason very well. They refuse to consider the consequences of their actions. The crack heads and geekers have got to be the worst. I can't imagine ever being stupid enough or down and out enough to try a drug like that. I might temporarily drink my way through a rough time but . . . really, crack? Talk about irresponsi-bility and making bad choices. I just don't get it.

SOBER THOUGHTS/QUERIES

Double Jeopardy

This smacks of double jeopardy. The addicted offender is indicted all over again: first (and justifiably so), for committing the crime and second, for even try-ing a drug in the first place! Many of us do play by the book. In an ideal world, none of us would ever take risks or experiment within our respective cultural envi-ronments. We would never try that first cigarette or that first warm beer. However, this is not an ideal world. For some, the decision to experiment with crack, when viewed in the context of a sea of bad choices and limited opportuni-ties, takes on a positive, almost survival quality.

Inhaling the Ecstasy . . . A Phenomenological Exercise

Crack cocaine—just imagine . . . euphoria on the rocks. Not from the bottle of cheap street wine but all within a mere eight seconds of putting down the pipe. The rock will crackle as the butane flame hits the screen, the vapors are released, and the lungs are charged. At that moment there are no worries, no problems, nothing but good feelings. There is virtually no time lapse. The high is immediate. Passionately described by users as the most intense high one could experience, here is one person's rendition:

> *The intensity of it was just so enormous, and I couldn't believe the rush. It was similar if not better than the rush we received from shooting it but you didn't have to put the holes in your arms. . . . The sensation starts in your head and goes down through your body. . . . It's very similar to an orgasm, the intensity of it.*[1]

We must come to believe in and, even more importantly, respect the intensity of the high associated with a particular drug. Crack is a good illustrative model because of its intensity. Far too often, the criminal justice professional is concerned only with the drug's basic illegality. Clearly, we cannot experiment personally with this drug, but we should have a deep phenomenological respect for its potential to induce euphoria.

Physicians are not required to undergo personal encounters with diabetes before they treat diabetics, nor are criminal justice professionals expected to experiment with crack (or any other drugs, including alcohol). The exceptional officer or counselor will seek to understand this phenomenon, convey as much to the addict, and avoid falling prey or "copping out" to the myth that only recovering professionals possess the knowledge and expertise to work with addicts. This is just not true. Be prepared to respond to such a challenge by the offender, but do not make matters worse by believing it.

Cultural Context

Understanding the cultural context of crack use (or any other drug use) is also critical. It is not used in a vacuum. Its intensity must be weighed against the user's socioeconomic and ethnic reality. A twenty-two-year-old poor and undereducated African American man from the inner city may experience a very different high (phenomenologically speaking) from his counterpart in white suburbia. This

---

1. D. Waldorf, C. Reinarman, and S. Murphey, *Cocaine Changes: The Experience of Using and Quitting* (Philadelphia: Temple University Press, 1991), 115.

was described eloquently by Jefferson Morley, writing in *The New Republic* (1989), when he chided the establishment for its own obsessive-compulsive relationship with materialism. How dare we vilify this drug without actually trying it? Morley dared to try it:

> *Crack is a pleasure both powerful and elusive. Smoke a rock and, for the next twenty minutes, you will likely appreciate sensuous phenomena ranging from MTV to neon lights to oral sex with renewed urgency. After your twenty minutes is up, you will have a chemical aftertaste in your mouth and, in all likelihood, the sneaking desire to smoke another rock— to see what that was really all about. Just one more. . . . You can be a moral tourist in the land of crack and still get a sense of how the drug can make sick sense to demoralized people. If all you have in life is bad choices, crack may not be the most unpleasant of them.[2]*

This is a provocative statement written by a presumably well-educated professional writer looking for answers to the crack problem from a firsthand, albeit risky, personal perspective.

Although crack use is not confined exclusively to the disenfranchised and has permeated the ranks of the middle class, we witness its use and abuse primarily by the less fortunate and more impoverished. Within this population and cultural setting, the choice to use crack could indeed become a dangerously alluring proposition, "if all you have in life is bad choices." Accepting this and trying to understand it may be the most important step we can take to help offenders recover.

We all have different attitudes, depending on the drug and why we think someone might try it in the first place. We all make bad choices in our lives, too. It does not mean we automatically turn into bad people simply because culture, peer groups, or other influences played a part in a decision to try an addictive chemical. An unaccepting and close-minded approach to the idea of experimenting with drugs in the first place only confounds our ability to establish a personal connection with the respective offender. Sound extreme? Think about it. Such a thinking pattern does nothing to enhance the supervision process.

How much difference is there between the street-level crack user who distorts and minimizes his use pattern and the probation officer who sits in his doctor's office and refuses to be honest about his own alcohol consumption? or food addiction? Isn't the probation officer, by his omission of information or slight

---

2. J. Morley, "What Crack is Like," *The New Republic* (2 October 1989).

twisting of detail, in effect saying that continuing to drink alcohol or eat abusively is more important, or has greater value to him, than his physical well-being?

Professional Humility: Not an Oxymoron

Community corrections workers are human beings. We, too, suffer from addiction; at the very least, 10 to 15 percent of us are alcoholic or drug-addicted. "They," our offenders, are also human beings. The only difference, in some cases, may be their addictive disease and the consequent symptomotology that ushered them into the criminal justice system. There is a "fine line between the keeper and the kept." Coming to terms with our own humanity, our own shortcomings, and our own susceptibility to making mistakes, we humble ourselves in a way that makes it possible to do effective work with offenders. It is nearly impossible to be simultaneously self-righteous and humble. Those of us who strive for this outlook have been known to say, "There but for the grace of God, go I." It is not a bad way to go.

Listen and Learn

Take the time to respect the offender's lifestyle, along with his or her cultural diversity. Offenders can and should be our best teachers. The process generates mutual respect and understanding, critical to the relationship as well as supervision goals. Ask questions about their life. What is it really like? What is happening on the street? What new drugs are out there? How do they see their addiction starting? What do they think will help them make a decision to ask for help? This is how we eliminate the "Bad Choices by Bad People" attitude.

COMPULSIVE LIARS
(or, the Power of Relapse and Denial?)

Those addicts are hopeless. They just don't get it. They start off with the best intentions, but before you know it they're back at it again. They don't care. The risk of jail means nothing; they seem incapable of making the connection between drug use and problems in their life. Sure, they'll clean up once, twice, but then inevitably they're off to the races and back to the joint. Talk about lying and distortion—just try to get a straight answer out of them. It's impossible. They tell me what they think I want to hear and nothing else, all the while rationalizing, minimizing, and flat-out lying to me. Ask them when they last used: they can't recall. Right—it was yesterday and they can't remember! Bull. Ask them how often they drink or get high, they'll tell you they aren't. Straight to your face, smelling like a vat of whiskey. How can I respect or trust a compulsive liar?

SOBER THOUGHTS/QUERIES

Falling Down on the Job

Those of us who subscribe to this line of thinking are not in an enviable career position. We do ourselves a great personal disservice by selectively or otherwise forgetting to acknowledge the offenders who *do* make it, with or without our help. All addicts are not hopeless. Some come awfully close, we admit. But they are in the minority, and usually, their deeper problem or coexisting disorder may not have anything at all to do with a primary addiction.

Many other offenders simply grow out of, get tired of, or mature through their addictions and criminal behavior. Nothing in this field is truly hopeless. We may feel hopeless. Our offenders may *feel* hopeless at times in their recovery. The community resources, government support, and formal treatment alternatives available to us may be woefully inadequate. Nevertheless, we must try to embrace hope and enthusiasm—in spite of the odds.

Trust versus Respect

Most of our working relationships with offenders are not two-way streets or pure counselor-client therapeutic alliances where trust is integral to the relationship from both sides of the desk. For example, we are not sure we should ever really trust offenders, regardless of their chemical dependency status. In the previous scenario we suspect the officer reacted a little too personally and started to lose objectivity as SRI attitude reared its head. To expect that an offender won't lie at times is a setup. Offenders have to work extra hard to earn our trust and respect. But we must, from the very beginning, do the best we can to engender their trust in us as professionals. We do this by always being respectable and trustworthy.

Dishonesty versus Denial

This can be a difficult distinction. After all, having to listen to the creative stories our offenders tell us all day long can wear us down. Perhaps this probation officer needed a refresher on the hallmark of addictive disease: denial. Denial comes in many disguises. It is often *not* dishonesty but actually what the offender truly believes! Technically, and in psychological jargon, it is a defense mechanism designed for self-protection. In order for offenders to continue this lifestyle of destruction, they must believe in it. Put yourself in their shoes and think about this: what would you do if your probation officer insisted that you stop drinking or using other drugs; demanded, in other words, that you stop doing the very thing, possibly the only thing, that seemed to have any value to you at all?

No Unsuccessful Interventions

There is no such thing as an unsuccessful intervention. Whatever happens, jail or treatment, relapse after relapse, it may all eventually be a part of the offender's "story" (as told in an AA or NA meeting) or somehow contribute to a meaningful "bottom," the consequence of which will be the decision to change. Keep the offender accountable. Jail can be very effective and therapeutic when used appropriately. Finally, consider the adverse effect of a potentially self-fulfilling prophecy of hopelessness (and helplessness) and how easy it is for us to unintentionally telegraph this directly to the offender.

Relapse Myths

Arnold Washton, an expert in treating chemical dependency, puts it best when he writes, "Relapse means that there is something wrong with the patient's recovery plan—not the patient."[3] Relapse also assumes that recovery has begun, that a period of abstinence has been achieved beyond superficial compliance.

This being the case, there are several relapse myths that must be challenged. Perhaps most damaging of all is the false assumption that relapse is a sign of poor motivation or treatment failure. This assumption reveals a certain naiveté about the very nature of addictive disease that will surely undercut any helping or monitoring effort. Change is very risky, and while some addicts may indeed be ambivalent about getting clean and sober, even the most highly motivated and sincere offenders can find themselves in the middle of relapse territory.

---

3. A. M. Washton, *Cocaine Addiction: Treatment, Recovery, and Relapse Prevention* (New York: W.W. Norton Co., Inc., 1989).

Treatment and recovery are all about learning from mistakes, developing better plans, recognizing relapse triggers, and applying relapse prevention methods. Relapses are not unavoidable. There is always a beginning, often a change in attitude or a stressful event that occurs well before an addict "picks up," followed by a progression of addictive thinking, poor choices, and finally, a snowballing of negativity that results in the decision to use again. This occurs sometimes months after the relapse actually began. *Returning to the drug of choice is the endpoint, not the beginning, of the relapse.*

MORAL WEAKNESS
(or, the Power of Addictive Disease?)

They are weak-willed. Absolutely. Whose choice was it to start using? No one forced heroin into their arm, coke up their nose, or a drink down their throat. And then, after getting in big-time trouble because of it, they still can't stop or even recognize it. If I ate apple pie and broke out in hives, I wouldn't come back for more, no matter how good it tasted. But the addicts do. Especially the street addicts. They have no motivation to improve themselves. Give them all the evidence in the world that they have a problem and they still go at it. Some of them have several priors. Some have good jobs, too, and still wind up losing them. Unbelievable.

SOBER THOUGHTS/QUERIES

Unbelievable, Unless . . .

It is absolutely unbelievable—unless, of course, you stay educated about the addictive process, you understand the dynamics of denial, the psychopharmacology of some drugs, and the totality of the spiritual malaise confronting the addict. And unless, in other cases, you understand the sociology of the street, the cumulative effect of the years of racism (at times subtle, at other times overt), and the powerful negative impact of differential opportunities for the disenfranchised. Poverty and unemployment, coupled with escalating anger and disillusionment within the ranks of the disadvantaged, create a formidable "occupational hazard," one that few of us have ever encountered, much less were challenged to overcome.

The Tough Questions, Again

If all you know is the street; if all you see are ex-cons with impressive jailhouse reputations; if your mother is an addict, your father unknown, and your uncle the corner drug dealer with a wad of cash and a reputation for getting high; if that is your "sociology," your home, and your worldview, aren't you somewhat of an anomaly if you *don't* get caught up in it? If you are human, and you do what your friends do, and you wind up in trouble with drugs or alcohol, where is the motivation to get yourself out of it? Where is the assurance that if you do get it together, embrace recovery, and stay clean, that the system will play fair with you? These are tough questions designed to help us remember what some of the harsh realities are that face offenders in their recovery.

Think about It . . . The Bum and the Brain Surgeon

Does moral weakness, the underlying tenet of implied choice, adequately explain how a bum on the street, living in complete squalor, chronically addicted to fortified wine, can look you in the face and deny that he has a problem? Has this poor soul, who used to be in mainstream society, made a conscious decision to exercise his morality by drinking himself to death? That is what makes no sense; this is what does not keep pace with rational thought or deductive reasoning—particularly when, after you examine this man and his day-to-day life, you realize the depth of his will to survive, despite all the odds. This man has character. He has intelligence and obvious willpower in many areas of his life. Yet the unenlightened might feel compelled to say his morals are so bad that he cannot stop drinking himself into oblivion. Who among us consciously chooses slow suicide?

Take the brain surgeon, the brilliant physician who underwent years of rigorous academic training to qualify for one of the most technically and intellectually challenging professions we know. He has the respect of his peers; he writes, publishes, and teaches medical school; he provides well for his family; and for many years he has received widespread public acknowledgment for his skills and expertise. Does this man suddenly make a *rational decision* to go "wrong" and jeopardize his career, family, and friends by virtue of a *moral weakness?*

This is a brain surgeon who we know for a fact has remarkable reserves of self-discipline, control, and sheer willpower. He must have. Look at what he accomplished. He exercised those reserves and realized important professional goals. Yet, despite this character strength and knowledge, he *allowed* himself to succumb to alcohol? Doubtful. Something larger than bad decisions or poor self-control led to this man's demise.

SO HELP-LESS
(or, Big-Time Enabling?)

I've just about had it with *those* addicts and alcoholics. You know me. I'll exhaust all possible treatment alternatives before I take them back to court or write for the warrant. This one guy, man, I was going out of my way to hook him up with all the right agencies, giving him breaks here and there, lending him small change, and authorizing "second chances." I mean, I went out of my way to help him start off on the right foot this time. He promised me over and over again that he was serious about getting himself clean. It's been six months, he's in full relapse again, and I'm really angry at him. But I won't give up or stop helping. He's got a fatal disease, called addiction. I'm fairly sure he's not committing new crimes for the drug money. Yet. I've put so much into this case. I know jail doesn't work. . . . I can really help him this time. I know I can.

SOBER THOUGHTS/QUERIES

Inverted SRI Attitude

An obvious degree of anger and frustration belies the "good" intentions expressed here. However, less obvious is the more subtle and yet possibly self-righteous presumption that somehow we (alone?) have the right stuff to bring the message of treatment to this addict. There is serious burnout risk inherent in such an attitude.

Our expectations for abstinence, for recovery, and for the entire treatment process may simply be at odds with the reality of an offender's capability to recover. Self-righteous indignation, as defined earlier, can take a shift and result in a narrow-minded expectation that someone will completely turn himself or herself around if given enough individual attention. This is hardly realistic for many of our cases that demand a team approach to the intervention process, up to and including longer-term therapeutic communities, competent outpatient contract aftercare programs, and transitional living arrangements.

Enabling versus Accountability: Don't Help

It must be obvious to most readers that what we have just discussed fits the category of "enabling." Offering treatment interventions ad infinitum, typically just for the sake of the officer's (or counselor's) mind-set, without attention to individual characteristics or needs, is not helping. We become increasingly frustrated and angry, all in the name of "helping." It is really not helping. We lose objectivity. The offender continues to manipulate the system to perpetuate his or her addiction. And no one is holding anyone accountable for anything. *Remember: Sending an offender to jail for continued substance abuse is precisely the right thing to do in certain circumstances.* This is true regardless of where we stand as criminal justice professionals on the social work-law enforcement continuum.

The skill—and this often takes years and many more mistakes to master (after all, this is an inexact science)—is knowing when jail or loss of freedom would be the most therapeutic intervention for a particular offender. We reach a point where experience tells us when not to help. We remain emotionally detached enough not to take any of it too personally. We remind ourselves that we did our best, that we tried to offer treatment alternatives designed to hold the individual accountable for recovery, but that perhaps it simply was not the time for this particular addicted offender to embrace abstinence. We hope that a valuable seed was planted.

Dual Disorders: Addiction Gets a Bum Rap

We know the bad news: Those addicted offenders who drive us crazy with anger and frustration. They don't get it, no matter how skillful and experienced we are, no matter what legal action may result. These are the individuals who seem, as the AA Big Book so aptly states, "constitutionally incapable of getting honest." Although we suspect that in reality they make up only a minority of the drug- and alcohol-addicted population as a whole, their negative impact is so pervasive that they feel like the majority. In effect, the goods are doubly damaged with this group. If we are not carefully discerning, addictive disease, in general, winds up getting a bum rap.

The suspicion is that this smaller but very hard to reach group of offenders are the ones who have cornered the market on our SRI attitudes, feelings of hopelessness, and general burnout. The danger is that we lose sight of chemical dependency as a treatable condition or disease. By virtue of the few really sick ones, it becomes something else altogether in a perceived exercise in futility. Some of these offenders do recover. We forget that for the general population who have addictive disease alone, recovery rates are often in the 60 to 70 percent range! Not a bad rate. Hardly futile.

It is important to understand that mental illness is often a coexisting disorder among the addicted offender population. When an offender is addicted to alcohol and drugs on top of a preexisting mental disorder, the challenge escalates: symptoms overlap, get intertwined and enmeshed. Which is causing which? How do you work through denial with someone who is characterologically impaired or even genetically predisposed to irresponsibility? Where is the leverage to work with these people? There is significant debate; there are many unknowns. Entire books have been written solely on how to prevent relapse with this particular population. What is going on in such a case is not simply the consequence of an independent addictive disease. It is surely not pure chemical dependency. It is the dramatic consequence of an addicted offender's *dual diagnosis* or *coexisting disorder.*

A person with a dual diagnosis has both a chemical dependency and a mental or emotional disorder. Oftentimes, however, the focus is on addiction and depression, or addiction and phobia, or addiction and anxiety disorder. But what about treating the addicted offender with a coexisting antisocial personality disorder? This population is rarely addressed. Not only are they in the minority among all chemically dependent people, but there is also less economic incentive for the treatment industry to intervene. Furthermore, they present an awesome clinical challenge to even the best and the brightest in the addictions field.

Terence Gorski, a well-known chemical dependency treatment practitioner and widely published author whose name today has become synonymous with relapse prevention, suggests that in some offender populations the incidence of antisocial personality disorder is not a minority phenomenon at all. Not surprisingly, antisocial behavior is common among criminal offenders. The normal population has about 4 percent of males and 1 percent of females who would fit the diagnosis of antisocial personality disorder. There are other groups of people, criminal offenders in particular, who he notes are at much higher risk than others. (See the following chart.)

Incidence of Antisocial Personality Disorder
All males..........................4%
All females............................1%
Alcoholic males.........................15%
Alcoholic females............................10%
Male narcotics addicts..........................32%
Prison inmates......................................50–80%[4]

Gorksi goes on to say that among chemically dependent criminal offenders, about 65 percent have both personality disorders and chemical dependency. His conclusion is that most habitual criminals have either serious personality disorders or criminal personality traits that in many cases are complicated by addiction. Gorski is convinced that punishment alone will not deter this population of offenders. He is a strong advocate of developing comprehensive treatment alternatives as a means of reducing criminal recidivism. *The fact that this group of coexisting disorders, especially the antisocial type, confounds the criminal justice system's response to treating addiction cannot be overstated.* It is a significant reality and challenges us all to avoid the temptation to give addiction treatment a bum rap.

A Conspiracy of Silence: On Alcohol

There has long existed a dangerous conspiracy of silence regarding alcohol. Of course, the silence is loudest within the alcoholic family: "We don't talk about Dad's drinking." But it also resonates on a higher level, within government agencies, within our society as a whole. "Drugs, drugs, drugs! It's crack, heroin, and speed that are tearing away the very fabric of our social institutions, destroying our

---

4. Terence T. Gorski, *Relapse Prevention Therapy with Chemically Dependent Criminal Offenders: A Guide for Counselors, Therapists, and Criminal Justice Professionals* (Independence, Mo.: Herald House, 1994).

families. Just say no to drugs!" Sound like a familiar battle cry?

The problem is this: We forget that alcohol is a drug. Beverage alcohol has become a mainstay of our social and economic culture. It is a legal drug for all of us over the age of twenty-one and a socially acceptable one for people a lot younger. Yet ethyl alcohol or ethanol remains a drug. In fact, it is a powerfully addictive toxic poison. A wise man once said that had the Food and Drug Administration (FDA) been around two thousand years ago when ethyl alcohol was first invented, it never would have approved of alcohol's casual dispensation at the typical American dinner table!

During Prohibition, alcohol was a "controlled substance" like many of the street drugs we see today. Contrary to popular thinking, prohibition actually worked. Statistics were convincing: deaths attributable to excessive drinking were way down. The point here is that alcohol is very much a drug with devastating societal consequences.

We forget this. We ignore the fact that alcohol is linked to 94,000 deaths a year versus the "mere" 21,000 fatalities attributable to other drugs. We need to be reminded that in total societal costs, alcohol is the heavy hitter, running up a bill exceeding $90 billion a year! Compare this to the $58 billion estimated to be the consequence of illegal drug use.

Addiction to alcohol is one of the primary public health problems in the United States today. Most would argue that it holds the number-two spot behind cancer. Were it not for the conspiracy of silence, it would probably be number one; so many deaths that are actually alcohol-related are not recorded as such. Because families would rather not risk disclosure, medical examiners and physicians do not always accurately report the true cause of death. Was it heart disease or alcoholism that led to the heart attack? We all know the scam.

The statistical facts are glaring. The average city police officer spends over half of his or her time on alcohol-related offenses. At least a third and probably closer to half of all men and women in prison are alcoholic or at least heavy drinkers. Alcohol is involved in 60 percent of the reported cases of child abuse and in the majority of domestic violence disputes. It causes more than 19,000 automobile fatalities a year. Alcohol is a central factor in divorce. Many would say that this drug either results in or triggers nearly half of society's most despicable crimes such as incest, child and spousal abuse, suicide, homicide, and various types of assault. Few would argue against its rather formidable position as the premier "gateway" drug used by children and adolescents prior to experimentation with harder drugs.

Mary Ann Barr, a respected clinical psychologist and consultant to the U.S. Probation Office for the Northern District of California, summarizes an exhaustive review of the academic and scientific literature on alcohol by writing[5]

- Alcohol has been shown to be repeatedly linked to aggression facilitation and criminal behavior.
- Alcohol use is highly correlated to all forms of family violence.
- Abstinence from alcohol is widely recognized in the private sector as the only realistic approach to alcohol dependence treatment.
- A significant proportion of drug-addicted persons also have undiagnosed alcohol dependency.
- Alcohol use has been shown repeatedly to be a major contributor to [other drug] relapse and the instigating event leading back to the addict's drug of choice.
- Alcohol use during or after drug treatment is related to poor outcomes in treatment. Commitment to absolute abstinence decreases the risk of a first slip.
- Abstinence from alcohol is consistent with the current therapeutic practices of drug and alcohol treatment in the private sector.
- For these reasons, abstinence from alcohol appears to be the only reasonable alternative in a high-risk population that has a demonstrated history of criminal activity, drug or alcohol dependence.

Gorski's numbers on alcohol use comparing the general population to the criminal offender population are quite revealing.

Alcohol Use in General Population
Abstainers......................33%
Nonproblem drinkers.............52%
Problem drinkers..........................15%

5. Mary Ann Barr, Ph.D., 2401 Marinship Way, Suite 300, Sausalito, CA 94965, as adapted from an unpublished paper.

Alcohol Use in Offender Population
Abstainers........................1%
Nonproblem drinkers.............29%
Problem drinkers..........................70%[6]

The disease of alcoholism shows little sign of easing its destructive impact. If anything, we suspect, it is on the rise as physicians, hospitals, and EAPs (Employee Assistance Programs) move toward more skillful recognition and diagnosis. It is even more obvious to those of us serving our communities as probation officers or contract drug treatment providers, particularly at the state or county level, where caseloads are likely to be dominated by persons convicted of alcohol-related driving offenses.

Nevertheless, the fact remains that most of us seem to prefer talking about, "staffing," or even supervising persons who abuse the illegal drugs like heroin, crack cocaine, or PCP. We operate from an accepted position of legality here where there is no confusion: a person abusing heroin is breaking the law. This is comfortable, known territory. However, it is fertile ground for various SRI configurations. Take phencyclidine (PCP), for example: "My God, who in their right mind would ever make such a stupid decision as to use an animal tranquilizer?" And so on. We hear it every day. We can all rally around the "scheduled" illicit drugs and feel comfortably superior and on target by "identifying out."

This is not so with the alcohol addict. And we use this term purposely so as not to make a distinction from other addicts. This unconscious avoidance of the problem is much more an issue with the alcoholic offender. Our personal feelings about alcohol, our experiences with family members, and even our own consumption patterns can pose significant distractions capable of sabotaging successful intervention efforts.

We can improve in this area, but not without significant change. We must develop a willingness to confront this unintentional but powerful pattern of avoidance. Sometimes we simply prefer not to bring up someone's drinking. We

---

6. Gorski, 17.

wonder if it is our business. We know the person will deny it, so why even bring it up in the first place? Perhaps we are just afraid to confront a suspected alcoholic—what will he or she say? Maybe we need better education about alcoholism, particularly interviewing and assessment skills, so that professional confidence could neutralize the fear.

We know what the reaction would be if a client smoked even one bowl of crack cocaine on probation, but what if he or she had a beer or two before a visit to the office or counseling session? What's the difference? How comfortable are we in this more nebulous arena? Maybe we feel pressed for time, that we really should focus our efforts on the illegal drugs and not waste time looking into someone's drinking. After all, whole families avoid the problem. Loving spouses overlook the pain or find a comfortable enabling pattern. Society as a whole allows alcohol to get lost in the fog created by the so-called illegal drug scourge. Why should we press on in the face of this reality?

We should press on because we occupy a unique position in society, somewhere along the continuum between the clergy and the police. By virtue of our potential for positive intervention and our obligation to serve the community, we ought to stand up to the challenge and counter these forces of avoidance. To do this, we have to push ourselves beyond the comfortable (or what we would like to believe about alcoholism) and into the midst of a serious reeducation process.

If we do not press on, we stand a good chance of missing the boat entirely. We will avoid making Twelve Step referrals or taking other action when we should. We will miss valuable intervention opportunities. Alcohol-related crime will continue unchecked. Alcohol-triggered relapses to illegal drugs of choice will proceed unabated. Alcohol-related driving fatalities and broken homes will continue to dominate the statistics. Let us do our small part to try and contain the problem by choosing not to perpetuate the conspiracy of silence on alcohol, by choosing not to ignore this other forgotten but far more damaging drug.

Disease versus Willful Misconduct

The reality is that we do not yet know what really causes alcoholism, or most other addictions for that matter. It is both sad and unfortunate, but we are simply not there yet. Wonderful strides in this direction have been made, but scientists are not able to predict with 100 percent certainty who will become dependent, under what circumstances, or on what drug. This should come as no surprise. There are hundreds, perhaps thousands, of conditions—environmental, psychological, and biological—that seem to defy complete and total explanation.

After all, what do we expect? How much scientific clarity can we reasonably count on? We covet true knowledge because it is the way we have been trained and educated all our lives, from grade school on. But how realistic are we being in this seemingly laudable pursuit? Even more important, how faithful to the truth are we when we do stumble on it?

There are those of us who get lost and dangerously sidetracked in this grand shuffle of words about what causes something. For some, the passion for having an explanation that makes complete sense is so strong that they miss the obvious. They would rather make up something than admit there may not be an absolute answer, yet. In scientific terms, the cause or origin of a disease or abnormal condition is called its *etiology.* There is significant ambivalence concerning the etiology of addiction. There seems to be two primary camps of thought. We will identify them as the "disease doubters" and the "disease promoters."

The disease doubters, a barely recognizable minority generally *not* found within the medical community, tout the writings of Herbert Fingarette. He is neither physician nor scientist but a research philosopher who promotes an antidisease model of addiction by making provocative statements. He stated in 1988, with no direct clinical experience of his own, that there really was no such thing as alcoholism. He delivered a stunning indictment of past and present alcohol research efforts by writing, "Despite decades of imminent breakthroughs, the current dominant consensus among researchers is that no single explanation, however complex, has ever been scientifically established as the cause of alcoholism."

Fingarette and some of his other nonmedical community supporters (Stanton Peele, Ph.D., included) suggest that we stop using the word *disease* and that after close examination we may all agree that reliance on such a word is but a crutch. Why? Because the essential basis of the argument is that alcoholism and other addictions are no more a disease than any other behavioral abnormality witnessed in the community. The disease doubters talk of evidence that genetics, for example, can be implicated in predisposing people toward a variety of disparate behaviors, including violence and superior intellectual achievement. So, they wonder, should we consider violence a disease and, therefore, exonerate murderers?

They proceed with further claims that the disease concept of alcoholism (and by natural extrapolation, addiction in general) has overextended its boundaries, perhaps even to the point of discrediting itself by falling prey to the business interests of insurance companies, treatment centers, and personal (i.e., self-serving) litigation efforts. The disease doubters are also the staunch moralists. They use the phrases "volitional act" and "willful misconduct" to describe alcoholism and other addictive disorders.

This line of reasoning is not without its temptations. It is clear. It is succinct. It is black and white. People get addicted to substances because of lifestyle differentiations, decisions about right and wrong (to use or not to use), and the individual need to escape reality. Willful misconduct, right? It is so obvious.

Not so fast. Those in the majority camp, the disease promoters, would say this type of reasoning is dangerously facile. They use the fact that many, if not all, physiological traits of alcoholism may be found within the nonalcoholic to underscore the presumably critical missing link: the absence of a direct and clearly distinct predisposing factor (genetic or otherwise) toward the disease itself. The fact that all alcoholics (or other addicts) do not necessarily follow the same route to dissolution implies, to the disease doubters, that alcoholism may not be a single, binary condition, whose etiology and prognosis would be entirely predictable. So what? This highlights the obvious, say the disease promoters, and moves us no closer to understanding the genesis of addiction.

So what is this debate all about? Perhaps it is about a very real sense of frustration at our not being able to identify a *single* medically scientific and proven cause for the disease of addiction. Because of this, goes the thinking of the doubter camp, how dare we refer to it as a "disease"? To the real clinical and medical treatment experts this does not present a problem. Disease is "dis-ease." Most of us would agree with Dr. Mark Gold when he writes that one of the most important medical discoveries of the twentieth century was that *"addiction is a disease"* (italics mine).[7] The problem is that it does not have one single cause. It is multifaceted. It is complex. And we do not fully understand it yet, nor do we fully understand the complex interrelationship between the mind (our brain, our spirituality) and the body. Scientists seem to be suggesting more and more frequently that the boundaries may not be at all clear. We must pause and reflect on our customary aversion to thinking holistically, always choosing to separate mind from body.

The semantics of the debate, however, distract us from the real problem. The reason there is disagreement, emotion, and conflict over the word *disease* in the first place is that the real focus should be on the word *responsibility.* This is the concept crouching in the shadows behind the word. It does deserve discussion.

As a society, we want desperately to hold people accountable for their actions. As criminal justice professionals, we must hold people accountable for their actions. It is our job. But how do we assign blame to the alcoholic or drug addict

7. Mark S. Gold, M.D., *The Good News about Drugs and Alcohol* (New York: Villard Books, 1991), 66.

who kills innocent victims on the highway? Who is the actual victim anyway? This is clearly where the communication process begins to erode.

In our opinion both are victims. The addict is a victim as well, even though he or she (and his or her disease) killed innocent people and even though his or her own victimization would rightfully be considered less harmful or egregious. Interestingly, this is precisely where we can begin to compromise (only a little) with the staunch moralists. We accept our responsibility to properly use legal authority to help the alcoholic or addicted victim begin the process of recovery. If he or she is unable to meet this goal or the resistance is too formidable, we are then responsible for initiating negative consequences for noncompliance, typically in the interests of community protection. It is our responsibility to help identify the problem for the victim of addiction and to help promote recovery as an option.

Then, *once identified as an addict,* it is the addicted offender's ultimate responsibility to seek and follow through with treatment recommendations. Consequently, we hold the offender accountable at this moment in time, just as we would the victim of diabetes or manic depression. We do not assign blame. However, we do expect a constructive treatment effort. And, as the case may be, we prosecute the addicted victim for his or her crime.

It is so tempting to try and make addiction a matter of personal choice, morality, willpower, or character strength because the issues are complex, the variables numerous, and the research incomplete at this time. We suggest that community corrections professionals learn to embrace the complexity of addictive disease and work from that basis.

Out of the C.A.G.E. and into Assessment

If we are to put aside the distracting debate about addiction-associated etiology, we cannot neglect the evaluation, diagnostic, or classification *process.* Ideally, of course, assessment should always be our priority as we work with our caseloads. But assessment is not static. It should be evolving all the time, throughout the life of a case. At times, we may seem to take one step forward, two steps back. As an offender's circumstances change, so too must our assessment to meet the needs of the individual case, whether it involves community protection issues or correctional treatment goals.

To best capture the definition of assessment and to appreciate its characteristic fluidity in our work is to understand that it simply means starting where the offender is. Obviously this will take sharp interviewing skills. We must gather personal information as well as a drug and alcohol history. We must find out who this person is, his or her attributes and shortcomings. Obviously, the drug history is critical to the overall assessment and vital to the intervention process. It also is one of the best ways to start the development of a workable relationship with the offender. Unfortunately, it also is an area requiring some caution. If we do not know what we are doing or convey significant anxiety about our subject matter (e.g., knowledge about drugs, street vernacular, and so on), we risk losing the confidence of the offender, which can then inhibit the integrity of the evaluation.

The fact is that underutilization of the chemical dependency assessment is an all too common occurrence within our profession. This results in significant losses on both sides. We lose out on the information we need to make good treatment recommendations. The addicted offenders lose out on the valuable clinical (and, one would hope, educational) interaction integral to the interview process. It is simply not sufficient to extract an admission of use and proceed to make referrals. We need facts. Contrary to popular belief, we need the offender's input. We can anticipate the denial, the distortion, and other defense mechanisms, but we must also realize that our skill in working through this is why we were hired in the first place. We are professionals, and it is our job to get beneath these defenses and extract information that will, over time, help us build and shape our assessment.

It is also not appropriate to rely solely on urinalysis records. Typically, they reveal only a snapshot of that person's relationship to a drug at the approximate time the drug was taken, not before, not since. For example, one positive result for an illicit drug, in and of itself, tells us absolutely nothing about whether or not that person is chemically dependent. We need historical data and perspective. Where has the offender been (vis-à-vis his or her drug use) and where is the offender right now? We need a detailed drug use history capable of making those fine distinctions between less severe drug *abuse* and out-of-control drug *dependency*. We may not all be experienced clinicians but we must learn to assess. Without an assessment, there is no starting point for referral, no chart for the course of treatment, and no content with which to confront the addict's denial system.

Out of the C.A.G.E. and into assessment? The word *cage* is an appropriate metaphor for where we are in the supervision process when we do not properly value assessment. At this point we are locked up, stymied. *If we do not know where we are, how do we know where we are going?* One of the most widely used, informal, and practical assessment screening devices is known as the C.A.G.E. Questionnaire. It is an acronym for Control, Anger, Guilt, and Eye opener. Designed historically for use in diagnosing alcoholism, the C.A.G.E. Questionnaire also turns it into an effective drug addiction screening tool with some small creative changes in wording.

The C.A.G.E. Screening Tool

1. Have you ever felt the need to *Control* or *Cut down* on your drinking or drugging?
   - Focus on the key issue of control, the loss of which (or a pattern thereof, at least) generally forms prima-facie evidence of addiction.
   - Do not ask open-ended questions, such as, "Do you think you might have a problem controlling your use of cocaine?"
   - With regard to alcohol, for example, ask about switching brands, vows to stop, resolutions to limit drinking during certain times, personal proscriptions against drinking in the car, alone, and so on.

2. Have you ever felt *Annoyed* or *Angry* in response to criticism of your drinking or drugging?
   - Ask if anyone close to the addict has ever expressed concern about his or her use pattern, e.g., spouses, lovers, siblings, children, or close friends.
   - How did the addict feel when that person voiced his or her criticism? Was the criticism at all warranted?

3. Have you ever experienced *Guilt* feelings when it comes to thinking about your drinking and drugging?
   - Would this person's overall quality of life be improved without alcohol, without so much alcohol, or without drug use?
   - Ask about waking up and feeling ashamed about the incidents of the night before, spending money the addict did not have, and so on.

4. Have you ever taken a morning *Eye opener* or felt it necessary to start your day with your drug of choice?[8]
   - This question is usually one that tries to determine how seriously chemically dependent a person might be.

Note: Answering yes to any one of these four questions implies that the offender is moving out of the experimental or early stage of use and certainly warrants further assessment beyond this general screening procedure. The C.A.G.E. questionnaire is recommended only as a broad screening device. It also lends an overall framework to the questions we need to get comfortable asking offenders.

---

8. Adapted from J. A. Ewing, "Detecting Alcoholism: The C.A.G.E. Questionnaire," *Journal of the American Medical Association* 252 (1984): 1905–7.

Final Comments

The impact of following these guidelines in conducting a drug history interview should be obvious. By patiently walking the offender through these questions and exchanging information in this way, we will be naturally induced to start forming a working relationship, one that extends beyond the "Do as I say" paradigm. Just as important, we will be laying the foundation for breaking through the denial system. The goal is to match the addict's current level of dependency with an appropriate treatment option. By determining specific patterns of use, relapse triggers, and losses associated with substance abuse or dependency, we can tailor a supervision plan to the individualized needs of the addict. Again, put even more simply, starting where the offender is becomes the focus. The ultimate beneficiary is not just the offender; your time and resources won't be wasted either. Everyone becomes a winner.

Into Action: "Raising the Bottom" with Positive Authority

We hear it all the time, inside and outside our offices: "You can't help addicts unless they want help." This thought pattern forms the basis of what is probably the single most erroneous and damaging misconception about addictions treatment, in general, and Twelve Step referrals, in particular. Sit in any AA or NA meeting and listen to the number of people who directly attribute their sobriety to someone or something outside of themselves that became the leverage point and "raised the bottom" for them. Father Joseph Martin, a well-known priest devoted to helping alcoholics, once said, "You can lead a horse to water, but you can't make him drink—but you sure can hold him there long enough to make him thirsty."

Patiently waiting for an offender to have a spontaneous eruption of internal motivation to seek recovery is both unrealistic and uninformed as it relates to the clinical essence of addictive disease. It is, after all, as we have stated earlier, the only disease that tells its victims they do not have it. Resistant drug- or alcohol-addicted offenders can get clean and sober even if they are not overtly motivated. No one ever walks into an NA or AA meeting without a sizable footprint on his or her back, whether it be from a spouse, employer, or probation officer. The motivation for recovery begins in treatment, rarely before.

Consequently, we are derelict in our duties if we do not try our utmost to mandate, direct, order, insist upon, cajole, or otherwise convince appropriate offenders to attend Twelve Step meetings. The disease of addiction, because of its progressive component, will not sit back passively and allow us the luxury of being reactive; we must actively and routinely hold addicted offenders accountable to their disease and, by natural extension, their responsibility to treat it.

The model we prefer to use as a paradigm for understanding what ought to be the criminal justice professional's role actually dates back to AA's early history. For years in AA, it was mistakenly held that alcoholics (and addicts) would be unable to initiate recovery unless a meaningfully "low bottom" had been achieved, in other words, complete personal devastation. Fortunately, AA has since changed its thinking. The bottom line now is that we must become bottom-raisers for addicted offenders. In other words, the therapeutic use of our court- or parole-sanctioned authority, in conjunction with our knowledge of the disease process, should mean the lowering of offender pain thresholds, the creation of discomfort by insisting upon complete abstinence, nonacceptance of "controlled drinking" behavior, possible returns to court for violations, and even jail. The result may be that decisive connection between continued drug use, tenuous court or parole status, and ultimate powerlessness over the drug.

Those of us uncomfortable with the therapeutic use of positive authority and confrontation as a supervision tool in working with this population will be put to the test. We must hone our skills in this area and learn to become able and confident professional interveners. This means taking on a number of different roles and executing a variety of different supervision tools. It means not avoiding the difficult questions about an offender's drinking or drugging habits. It means taking the time to get specific and draw the offender out during the ongoing assessment process. We are talking about forced enlightenment here, and it will come much easier to us if we're convinced we are relating to someone with a bona fide addiction and not a circumstantial abuse problem.

Therapeutic use of positive authority means initiating a good urinalysis program, including random drops. It means acting on a hunch about pursuing someone's possible relapse, even though it may result in more work. It means sloshing through the denial, not accepting it, and keeping your word about graduated treatment sanctions. It means not being afraid to persist in a line of questioning on a drug-positive follow-up even though you want to believe the offender's explanation. It means holding the offender accountable to his or her Twelve Step meeting regimen, to professional outpatient counseling, and other supervision-related obligations. It means getting to the point where offenders actually know that it is their *disease* you do not trust, not them personally. It means learning about relapse prevention and how to spot one in the making, even before the drug is picked up. In some cases, of course, it will also mean knowing when to use imprisonment as a therapeutic response or ultimate bottom-raiser.

Terence Gorski put it simply when he wrote, "Mandated clients often have higher long-term recovery rates than voluntary clients. This is because when the going gets rough and they want to drop out of treatment, they can't. They have to stay in treatment and work through the tough issues that will allow them to have meaningful and comfortable lives of sobriety."[9] Mandated treatment, including mandated attendance at self-help group meetings, works.

9. Gorski, 34.

CHAPTER 3

First Things First:
Understanding History through Tradition

In Retrospect: From Then to Now

An active member of AA today, cautiously hopeful that a new acquaintance may also be in recovery (and perhaps AA), might interrupt a casual conversation and interject, "Are you a friend of Bill Wilson's?" If the answer is "yes," it often precipitates an immediate bond of mutual understanding. "No" means nothing more than an uncomfortable moment before the conversation goes wherever it was going in the first place. This simple query has become a universally accepted way of anonymously finding out whether someone you do not know may also be a member of AA.

William Griffith Wilson, known in AA circles as "Bill W.," was the co-founder of this phenomenal organization that had its beginning in Akron, Ohio, during May of 1935. Wilson, a man torn between paradoxical extremes, was a hopeless alcoholic who had experienced numerous unsuccessful hospitalizations. In November of 1934 he was in a New York City hospital when he had what he described as a "spiritual experience"; he never drank again and died sober at the age of seventy-five on January 24, 1971.

Wilson was a bright man, a Wall Street hustler; he was smooth, charismatic, terribly passionate and sensitive, and, yet, also painfully egocentric and self-centered. This last drinking episode in November did not mark AA's birth, however. That happened several months later when he found himself on business in an Akron, Ohio, hotel, still dry, but very depressed. He was a stranger in a strange city with much too much spare time on his hands before returning home. To make matters worse, his cravings escalated as he heard the enticing sounds coming from the hotel bar. Inexplicably, he suddenly thought the best defense against taking a first drink would be to find another alcoholic with whom he could talk.

Having been exposed to the Oxford Group, a sort of spiritual predecessor of AA, Wilson had learned that an alcoholic will listen to another alcoholic talk about what they both know best: booze and trouble. He made a few phone calls and eventually met "Dr. Bob" Smith, another "hopeless" and still drinking alcoholic in the area. Wilson made it through without a drink, reinforcing his growing conviction that he alone could not stay sober and that he needed the help only another alcoholic could provide.

"Dr. Bob," as he is called, had his last drink on June 10, 1935, the day AA officially recognizes as its beginning. The story has it that it was Wilson who handed the surgeon his last bottle of beer that day before an operation. Although atypical for most recovering alcoholics, Dr. Bob was one of the unfortunate few who was never completely able to shake the compulsion to drink; he experienced some form of it every day for fifteen years, until his death in November of 1950. His last words to Bill, muttered with a wink, were: "Remember, Willie, don't louse it up. Keep it simple."

AA became Alcoholics Anonymous in 1939 when the "Big Book" (entitled *Alcoholics Anonymous)* was first published. By 1939 there were only a hundred "ex-drunks" working to keep themselves sober, not exactly a ground swell. But Wilson and other early AAs did not "louse it up," and by 1944 membership had grown to 10,000. By 1971 it had grown to 500,000, and the present-day participation level is said to be well over two million. Some now say that AA doubles its membership every decade, clearly a testament to the fact that this grassroots movement has no intention of fizzling out, that it is not a fickle phenomenon subject to the winds of time. It is here to stay, to grow and flourish for our children as well as our children's children, and beyond.

It has now been well over half a century since that small band of "hopeless" alcoholics began their journey into what eventually became the fellowship of Alcoholics Anonymous, recognized today as the most successful antidote to alcoholism. The core literature, the Twelve Steps and Twelve Traditions, and the beauty of how it works one day at a time have not changed at all since then. What has changed is the sheer number of people involved today and the general public's perception about alcoholism in particular and drug addiction, in general.

Although there are more than two million active AA members today, there are undoubtedly millions more unaccounted for who pass through its doors and begin a healing process that results in lasting change. These scores of people are not "officially" counted by AA because they do not attend meetings regularly. There are also countless others (spouses, children, and friends) who are secondarily impacted by someone else's AA involvement. Any way you look at it, AA has cut a large swath into mainstream society. Couple this with the astronomical growth of other Twelve Step-oriented offshoot groups and we have a bona fide twentieth-century social phenomenon.

There are two major historical ramifications, perhaps less immediately obvious but no less important, attributable to AA's growth and development over the years. The first has to do with the general public's growing awareness of addiction as a medical disease. The American Medical Association declared alcoholism a progressively fatal disease in 1956, further validating AA's etiological opinion about the condition and definitely swelling its membership ranks. One of AA's classic trademarks is the notion that the alcoholic suffers a disease, a "physical, mental, and spiritual" disease for which there is no known cure. As they say in AA, alcoholics are "sick people getting better," not "bad people getting worse." The alcoholic learns to accept responsibility for recovery from the disease but not to wallow in self-loathing for having it in the first place.

AA has done much to harness the shame, guilt, and stigmatization traditionally associated with chemical dependency, and all within the spirit of anonymity. Nothing has ever been carried out in the official name of AA—no grandstanding, in other words. Take, for example, passage of the Americans with Disabilities Act, which was due in no small part to AA's profound influence. It has a legislative impact resulting in noticeable compassion and understanding for the complexity of addictive disease.

The second historical consequence has to do with the birth of today's so-called treatment industry. Professional treatment resources for alcoholics and addicts have not always been so plentiful. Although managed care, health insurance reform, and the harsh reality of the domestic economy will always place us at the mercy of change, a variety of resources do exist today that were conspicuously absent prior to AA's emergence. The professional counselors are there to help; recovering paraprofessionals are there to assist; drug and alcohol programs, treatment centers, and "rehabs" pepper our larger communities. There are twenty-eight- and ninety-day programs, longer-term therapeutic communities, social detox programs, and intensive outpatient group counseling regimens. Physicians, social workers, community corrections staff, psychologists, psychiatrists, and ex-offenders alike are seeking certification, and in some cases licensing, as addictions specialists. The field of addictions counseling has carved itself a significant and well-respected niche within the health care system.

AA did not purposely engineer *any* of this. Remember: AA has no opinion or official involvement on any outside issue. Therein lies the beauty of AA and why, paradoxically, it has probably had more far-reaching impact than any other organization devoted to helping the alcoholic. AA avoids controversy and, at the public level, maintains its humility in a way that builds trust. The trust, and resulting respect it fuels, seeps into mainstream society, thereby affecting people's opinions about and attitudes toward addiction.

"Upside Down" Anarchy: Understanding the Traditions

Unlike the typical American business, whose organizational flowchart starts with the CEO and his or her boardroom situated at the top of the triangular schematic, whereby directives flow downward, AA and many other Twelve Step groups are managed in just the opposite manner. Each meeting and each area group of meetings actually runs its own show completely. No one person or central group is in charge.

What emerges schematically is an inverted triangle with headquarters, or the General Service Office (GSO) of AA in New York City, recommending and suggesting, but not mandating, what should be carried out at the group level. There are no executive officers, formal leaders, or supervisors with any special authority; there are only "trusted servants."

How does it work? What's the bottom line that holds this incredible, almost anarchist, "nonorganization" organization together? It is all about the Twelve Traditions. Here they are in full, AA's central nervous system:

The Twelve Traditions of Alcoholics Anonymous[1]

1. Our common welfare should come first; personal recovery depends upon AA unity.

2. For our group purpose there is but one ultimate authority—a loving God as He may express Himself in our group conscience. Our leaders are but trusted servants; they do not govern.

3. The only requirement for AA membership is a desire to stop drinking.

---

1. The Twelve Traditions of AA are taken from *Twelve Steps and Twelve Traditions,* published by Alcoholics Anonymous World Services, Inc., New York, N.Y., 129–87. Reprinted with permission. (See editor's note on copyright page.)

4. Each group should be autonomous except in matters affecting other groups or AA as a whole.

5. Each group has but one primary purpose—to carry its message to the alcoholic who still suffers.

6. An AA group ought never endorse, finance, or lend the AA name to any related facility or outside enterprise, lest problems of money, property, and prestige divert us from our primary purpose.

7. Every AA group ought to be fully self-supporting, declining outside contributions.

8. Alcoholics Anonymous should remain forever nonprofessional, but our service centers may employ special workers.

9. AA, as such, ought never be organized; but we may create service boards or committees directly responsible to those they serve.

10. Alcoholics Anonymous has no opinion on outside issues; hence the AA name ought never be drawn into public controversy.

11. Our public relations policy is based on attraction rather than promotion; we need always maintain personal anonymity at the level of press, radio, and films.

12. Anonymity is the spiritual foundation of all our traditions, ever reminding us to place principles before personalities.

There are very few recovering addicts and alcoholics who, in sharing their story, will not emphasize the significance of their early understanding of the Traditions. The Traditions make it clear to the newcomer, usually through the interpretive eyes and ears of someone with more experience in the program, that the program is not religious; that it does not work for social services or anyone else, for that matter; and that it does not have the authority or interest to tell anyone what to do or how to behave. No, they will not report back to the authorities.

The reality is that AA, and the other Twelve Step groups in general, are as widely misunderstood as the disease itself. If we are to be successful in making a referral, we must be qualified to sell the product, often a hard sell, as it turns out. It takes finesse and considerable skill to reinterpret the facts, to make them clear and understandable to the offender. This is not to suggest that we must explain in specific detail how the program works. (Even AAs will shun such queries—"It just works," they say). What it does require is basic knowledge of what AA is and is not. It does ask us to get comfortable using the many techniques (the most important of which is accurate information!) at our disposal to dispel the myriad twists of false information, innuendo, and stereotype that inevitably shroud the Twelve Step programs in the mind of the addicted offender.

Protecting the Fellowship: In Twelve Ways

The Twelve Traditions are to the Fellowship as a whole what the Twelve Steps are to the individual in recovery—they protect. If honestly followed as guidelines, they guarantee progress and health for the Fellowship. Were it not for the Traditions and the AA resolve to remain within their boundaries over the years, the Fellowship would not survive. The individual recovering addict or alcoholic follows the Steps, works his or her own personal program from the inside out, and as part of his or her obligation to the larger group (or meeting), abides by the Traditions. Each and every person works simultaneously for the good of the whole and himself or herself personally. This is quite effective. Certainly time-tested.

Unless otherwise noted, the various quotes and most of the historical background information pertaining to each Tradition has been taken from AA's second most widely read publication, the *Twelve Steps and Twelve Traditions* (or the "Twelve and Twelve"). The "Interpretive Referral Notes" are designed to provide the reader with additional practical or supervision-oriented technical insight.

The First Tradition: Unity versus Individualism

> *Our common welfare should come first; personal recovery depends upon AA unity.*

No person can compel another; no member can punish another; and no one possesses the power to expel. In fact, the Twelve Traditions do not contain a single "don't." Central to this tradition is the notion that the recovering alcoholic requires a group within which to "carry the AA message" or "pass it on" (see Step Twelve); he or she needs other group members or alcoholics to stay sober and, ultimately, to stay alive. By learning to live together as a group and respecting the rights of each individual member (almost to the point of anarchy), AA as a whole will survive the damaging forces of "personalities destroying whole peoples." If the group does not survive, neither will the individual alcoholic member.

> **Interpretive Referral Notes:** This cuts to the very core of the program's efficacy for the offending population, which is not known for trusting

institutions. There really are no directives, only suggestions. Of course, this runs counter to what most offenders expect and what most criminal justice professionals do best: issue instructions and directives.

The Second Tradition: Who's in Charge?

For our group purpose there is but one ultimate authority—a loving God as He may express Himself in our group conscience. Our leaders are but trusted servants; they do not govern.

The answer to this question of who is in charge is open-ended and left up to full individual interpretation. It is "God, *as we understood Him,*" not God according to any one person or religion. The fact that AA has no president with ultimate authority, no treasurer able to compel dues payment, and no board of directors would be confusing to anyone. AA's early experiences with the traditional one-person leadership model, general principles of democracy, and a group's "hierarchy of service" highlighted serious problems with all three constructs. These failings reinforced and ultimately gave birth to the notion of "group conscience" as the guiding program reality. So it was written, "This is the experience which has led us to the conclusion that our group conscience, well-advised by its elders [respected old-timers], will be in the long run wiser than any single leader." And in response to a question about whether or not AA has real leadership, it is cleverly (or paradoxically) written: "Most emphatically the answer is 'Yes,' notwithstanding the apparent lack of it."

> **Interpretive Referral Notes:** Although the "loving God" phrase and the obvious importance placed on the spiritual context may initially disturb some adamant nonbelievers, we must stress the prohibition against government. Emphasize over and over that no one person is in charge— "You [the offender] are just as much a part of how the group decides to evolve as the person sitting next to you who's been around twenty years!" Stress the antiauthority theme; talk about the peculiar freedom this allows and the degree to which these groups defy mainstream laws of government.

The Third Tradition: Who Can Attend?

The only requirement for AA membership is a desire to stop drinking.

AA members leading off a meeting may choose to begin their opening remarks by "qualifying." This refers to the reasons they are qualified to declare themselves a member of the Fellowship. Actually, such a detailed qualification or story is completely unnecessary. You are a member of the Fellowship when you decide you are. It is as simple as that.

The literature points out that historically it took years to arrive at this wonderfully pragmatic approach to membership requirements. Groups used to have membership rules, or "protective regulations," as they were called. By their own admission, and largely because early AA members were convinced they had finally stumbled on their salvation, they were worried sick about the group's survival if "beggars, tramps, asylum inmates, prisoners, queers, plain crackpots, and fallen women" were allowed entrance. Time changed this doctrine, and experience finally eroded their initial attempts to exclude people.

Two scenarios about the historical development of this Tradition are discussed in the Twelve and Twelve and warrant mention. The first addresses dual addiction, noted as a "double stigma," and the early group members' struggle over whether or not to admit the dually addicted, or, as we would say now, those with a cross-addiction. We suspect, although it is not mentioned specifically, that they were alluding to the latter, such as a narcotics addict who also happened to want to stop drinking. The group eventually opened its arms, after quite a bit of contentious debate.

The second scenario takes on the "God" question. An alcoholic salesman wanted to become a part of the Fellowship. The only trouble was that he was staunchly and unabashedly atheist. When confronted, he reminded them of their own words, written at the time in the foreword to the Big Book, that stated the only requirement for membership was a desire to stop drinking. He stayed in the group. Eventually, he got drunk but later returned, more open-minded about his spirituality.

Finally, it should be pointed out that this Tradition does not say the requirement is "to stop drinking." Most AAs admit they never would have come to their first meeting had this been the case. Although it is an abstinence-based fellowship, a still-drinking member will not be removed unless he or she is disruptive to the group. What is important is the desire, the inclination, not the act itself.

Interpretive Referral Notes: This is an important and somewhat tricky Tradition: We must simultaneously stress the fact that Twelve Step meetings are abstinence-based and, yet at the same time, be able to encourage someone who isn't quite there yet to get there anyway. There will also be times when offenders resist attendance at closed meetings because they are not sure they really are alcoholics, or addicts. Talk it out; remind the offender that a simple desire not to drink or drug is sufficient qualification. Note how welcoming this Tradition is; the "minorities" within AA, including, for example, atheists and agnostics, belong just as much as anyone else.

The Fourth Tradition: Autonomy with a Caveat

Each group should be autonomous except in matters affecting other groups or AA as a whole.

AA's infatuation and obvious success with upholding the tradition of autonomy accounts for the incredible multiplicity and individuality of groups. There are almost as many different types of groups (see chapter 5) as there are members. The goal is to find the right "fit."

The caveat, "except in matters affecting other groups or AA as a whole," addresses a fundamental limitation as to how far-out a group or meeting might become. Historically, the lessons learned in this arena date back to an attempt to construct an AA-sponsored alcohol rehabilitation center. It was built, along with rules, regulations, and corporate bylaws. However, with the passage of time, "confusion replaced serenity," as dissension and trouble mounted on all fronts. The group eventually, and wisely, concluded that they had no business handling such a project.

> **Interpretive Referral Notes:** The AA or NA group itself is the key component to most newcomers' sustained sobriety in the Fellowship. The key is not, for instance, the literature or a specific institution. If it were that simple then all we would have to do is issue the right reading material or refer to the right facility, sit back, and wait for recovery to kick in. Rather, the focus is on one addict helping or talking to another. And since autonomy allows for so many "different meetings for different folks" (depending on geography, of course), it is our responsibility to do our best to ensure that addicted offenders get to the best meetings for themselves.

The Fifth Tradition: No Hidden Agendas

Each group has but one primary purpose—to carry its message to the alcoholic who still suffers.

AA operates within a completely nonprofessional context, not relying on anyone's particular "learning, eloquence, or on any special individual skills." This forms the basis for an organizational value system. Each group's purpose is clearly delineated by the boundaries inherent in the simple act of one alcoholic helping another.

This singleness of purpose is the great paradox of AA in that unless alcoholics and addicts get to the point where they can give their sobriety freely to others, they will not stay sober themselves. It also cuts to the core of AA's unwillingness to delve into matters of religion. Nor are AA groups interested in proselytizing for any other person, place, or thing, no matter how outwardly laudable or appealing. AAs really strive to, as they say, "keep it simple" and focus on carrying their message of hope from one alcoholic to the still suffering alcoholic.

> **Interpretive Referral Notes:** There are many misleading rumors about what AA meetings are like. Keep this in mind when discussing the topic with a potential newcomer. Offenders are typically misinformed and will try to rationalize their way out of Twelve Step meetings by harping upon such rumors. Do not buy it. Be prepared to explain this Tradition and reinforce the fact that AA does not care about where they work, how much money they make, or their value system. AA is only interested in having them share their experience about not drinking, if, in fact, they are courageous enough to open up and express as much.

The Sixth Tradition: No Endorsements

> *An AA group ought never endorse, finance, or lend the AA name to any related facility or outside enterprise, lest problems of money, property, and prestige divert us from our primary purpose.*

Historically, this Tradition began with AA's discovery that trying to be all things to all people would eventually threaten the Fellowship's very survival. Early AA groups (1930s through late 1940s), so enthusiastic about their success with the program, started thinking about and experimenting with rather grandiose notions of restructuring laws, getting into politics, and enticing the criminal justice system to parole offenders directly to their custody. In fact, AA did get involved, for a time, in the hospital business; it did not work. Things bogged down as the idealism ran smack into the reality of politics, money, and other conflicting causes. Similar bruising experiences only hardened AA's resolve to stay out of the endorsement arena.

> **Interpretive Referral Notes:** Even AA "clubs" and Twelve Step-oriented halfway houses or transitional homes (Oxford Houses, for example) make sure they do not publicly identify themselves with AA. The Fellowship does not administer these groups in any way, despite the fact that almost all participants are AA or NA members.

The Seventh Tradition: No Dues, Only Expenses

> *Every AA group ought to be fully self-supporting, declining outside contributions.*

Money took its toll, wreaking havoc with pioneer AA groups. Contributions. Donations. Benefactors. How were these groups to deal with the public's enthusiasm over their success? They wondered whether or not it was possible to mix AA and money. At one point it appeared as though individual recovering members began to prosper while AA "stayed broke." Outside interference began to resemble influence-peddling. Some groups were so frightened by these complications that they refused to keep any money in their treasuries.

Perhaps the best example of AA's struggle in this regard came after a woman's death and her sizable gift to the Fellowship. The General Service Office declined to accept it, declaring that AA "must always stay poor." Not surprisingly, local editorials and the media expounded on how the "irresponsible had become responsible"; how by making financial independence a part of its tradition, AA "had revived an ideal that its era had almost forgotten." Clearly, this was good press for a fledgling movement!

> **Interpretive Referral Notes:** There are no dues or fees for AA membership; it costs nothing to belong. When a member, typically at the half time of a meeting, says there are no dues or fees but there are expenses, and passes the basket, a $1 contribution is customary. Group expenses are usually as follows: "rent," [2] a supply of AA literature, contributions to local service groups, and the coffee fund. Sometimes they will encourage the "down and out" to take a dollar out of the pot!

The Eighth Tradition: AA is Nonprofessional

Alcoholics Anonymous should remain forever nonprofessional, but our service centers may employ special workers.

AA does not mince words on this one. "Alcoholics Anonymous will never have a professional class. . . . We have discovered that at the point of professionalism, money and spirituality do not mix." To get into the professional realm would defeat AA's singleness of purpose—one alcoholic helping another with no strings attached. Comparatively speaking, this Tradition did not take as long to cement. It did not take long to realize that the money motive would not work with the alcoholic. He would see right through it before the helper even uttered a word. However, this Tradition was very controversial within early AA circles. The debate centered around anyone making money from AA, up to and including General Service Office (GSO) janitors, secretaries, and those who hired themselves out to corporations as employee assistance practitioners.

---

2. Most groups will insist on paying some amount in rent despite gratuitous offers—AA is "fully self-supporting, declining outside contributions."

In the end it was determined that Twelfth Step work was the bottom line, the delineating variable. One could not, within the confines of his or her personal AA affiliation, be paid as a professional worker to pass on the message to another recovering alcoholic. So when it comes to managing contacts throughout the world, processing literature and publication demands, and handling the significant administrative responsibilities, AA will only employ "special workers" or staff, some but not all of whom are recovering themselves. These AA employees at GSO headquarters are not practicing the Twelfth Step. They are not leading or directing or professionally sponsoring anyone. They are simply "special workers."

> **Interpretive Referral Notes:** With regard to AAs who have gone to work for hospitals, employee assistance programs, and other rehabilitative enterprises, an important distinction is made between anonymity and professionalism. As long as a person is not getting paid to do Twelfth Step work, the tradition of non-professionalism remains intact. However, and this is known colloquially as "wearing two hats," there are inherent challenges in negotiating the potential pitfalls associated with being in the program and working as a paid counselor. How much personal disclosure to the client is warranted? How do you avoid sponsoring that person instead of professionally counseling him or her? Where do you draw the line? Keeping professionalism and Twelfth Step work separate forms the core of this Tradition.

The Ninth Tradition: Organized Freedom

AA, as such, ought never be organized; but we may create service boards or committees directly responsible to those they serve.

As discussed earlier, AA does not conform to mainstream organizational management schemes. Committees may be organized but they do not run or direct anything. No group can expel or punish a member. No one can tell someone to stop working with this or that particular person. No single AA hotshot at the GSO in New York has any authority either. This is not to say that GSO headquarters is silent on issues affecting AA. They make plenty of suggestions.

AA quickly recognized that "alcoholics can't be dictated to—individually or collectively." The directives, calls for obedience, and the principles necessary for continued existence as an organization must come *from within the spiritual reserves of the individual member.* And so it is written, "AA has to function, but at the same time it must avoid those dangers of great wealth, prestige, and entrenched power which necessarily tempt other societies. . . . Tradition Nine . . . discloses a society without organization, animated only by the spirit of service—a true fellowship" (Twelve and Twelve, 175).

The Tenth Tradition: None of Our Business

Alcoholics Anonymous has no opinion on outside issues; hence the AA name ought never be drawn into public controversy.

AA has done itself a tremendous favor by so skillfully staying out of other people's business. Having "no opinion on outside issues" means not getting into public controversies or taking positions. Try to debate religion, politics, or other controversial topics within an AA meeting. It usually won't happen. If someone does manage to initiate an unwarranted topic, an "old-timer" will either interrupt on the spot or entertain some polite counsel after the meeting. Of course, the transgressor will not be booted out; extemporaneous education about the Tradition's historical significance will likely suffice. By functioning so well at the individual level, the Traditions also work for the Fellowship as a whole.

Because of AA's "deep instinct" to stay out of the fight, "even a worthy one," the Fellowship has a much greater chance of continued survival and growth. Perhaps AA learned from the example of the Washingtonian Society, which started out much like AA. Composed of a group of alcoholics trying to help one another during the Civil War era, it evolved into a temperance society, allowing politicians and other outsiders to become involved. Since abolition of slavery was an issue of the day, members took sides on this, as well. It wasn't long before the s.ociety lost complete effectiveness in helping alcoholics.

The Eleventh Tradition: Attraction versus Promotion

Our public relations policy is based on attraction rather than promotion; we need always maintain personal anonymity at the level of press, radio, and films.

As described earlier, AA began in 1935 with two recovering alcoholics, Bill Wilson and Dr. Bob Smith. Today, it is estimated that there are at least two million active members throughout the world. Obviously, AA has had a successful public relations policy, though not from the very beginning. It evolved, as most of the Traditions have, over time and in spite of many painful experiences. This Tradition's core principle is at odds with customary public relations practice. AA found they had to rely on *"attraction rather than promotion."* This translates into not going out and publicly extolling the virtues of the Fellowship, or promoting individual personalities who have recovered in AA, or publicly advertising success stories in general. Personal anonymity was to become *the* guiding factor at the level of "press, radio, and films." Humility and self-restraint obviously paid off.

> **Interpretive Referral Notes:** Especially astute offenders may charge that this Tradition has been violated with some frequency. They would be right, unfortunately. Since the influx of entertainment and sports celebrities into treatment centers, there have been numerous examples of program members not remaining anonymous. Who knows? This unsolicited advertisement may have pricked up a few ears. But the fear is that "Mr. Famous" will turn around tomorrow and just as publicly relapse. What does that say about the program's efficacy, especially to the already cynical alcoholic? The founders of AA believed that undue publicity, good or bad, might possibly discourage newcomers from giving the program a try.

The Twelfth Tradition: Principles before Personalities

Anonymity is the spiritual foundation of all our traditions, ever reminding us to place principles before personalities.

The early groups and meetings of recovered alcoholics were kept very secret. Newcomers could only locate the "secret societies" through trusted friends; even though technically sober, recovering people nonetheless feared the "public distrust and contempt" they might face by coming out. Better to keep quiet about it.

There was also fear that a large influx of people to the program might threaten everyone's anonymity. As groups flourished and multiplied, the problem of anonymity took on increasing complexity. Gossip, at first seemingly well-intentioned, made for an early lesson in this regard. As the Twelve and Twelve states, "Clearly, every AA member's name—and story, too—had to be confidential, if he wished. This was our first lesson in the practical application of anonymity." Other problems developed when overly zealous newcomers began shouting about their sobriety and how influential AA had been for them, only to relapse and let down their respective groups.

So the question became, how anonymous should an AA member be? It would be fine for newcomers to make the choice to share with their spouse, doctor, minister, and close friends the fact that they had found a new way of life. Such "quiet disclosures" could help them surmount the stigmatization of their disease *and* discreetly spread the news of AA's availability. The founding members consented that though these disclosures were not in the "strict letter of anonymity," they "were well within its spirit" (Twelve and Twelve, 186).

This remained very limiting. AA needed more than word of mouth to grow. Open AA meetings, in which family, friends, or anyone just interested in AA could come see what it was all about, began to surface as means of filling the void. They did very well. Groups received requests for speakers to appear before a variety of community organizations and businesses. And "provided anonymity was maintained on these platforms, and reporters present were cautioned against the use of names and pictures, the result was fine."

AA had its day of reckoning when it stood firm to the increasingly seductive solicitations of major film, radio, and television companies. They were hungry for stories, and AA realized it could go either way and do "incalculable good or great harm." It was decided the risk would not be worth it. For the press, radio, and television, total anonymity would have to be the rule: "principles above personalities," *without exception.*

> **Interpretive Referral Notes:** This Tradition contains the real meaning of anonymity, which, contrary to popular belief, does not focus exclusively on preserving confidentiality or protecting someone from potentially damaging stigma should an employer, friend, or someone else find out about one's involvement. What it does do is spotlight the need to protect its members from using the Fellowship for personal gain, for realizing rewards or benefits as a consequence of being in the program. Personal gain strikes at the very heart of humility and often seduces people away from the group's ultimate purpose: "to stay sober and help other alcoholics to achieve sobriety." Nonetheless, both AA and NA are, as a rule, excellent about respecting personal anonymity in the more popular sense alluded to earlier.

Narcotics Anonymous Comes of Age: A Brief History

As strange as it may seem, one of the better-known noontime Narcotics Anonymous (NA) meetings in our nation's capital takes place *inside* the U.S. Courthouse for the District of Columbia, off the waiting area for the federal probation and parole office. This bona fide NA meeting thrives in the midst of the very same halls traversed by federal judges, high-powered assistant U.S. Attorneys, and myriad law enforcement agencies, some of whom may have locked the offenders up in the first place. Participants are government professionals, blue-collar workers, courthouse employees, and ex-offenders. Some of the ex-offenders are "on paper," referred directly by their probation officer. Others are "off paper," coming on their own—a fascinating mixture of backgrounds, socioeconomic status, and overall cultural diversity. All are there in pursuit of the same goal, despite widely divergent backgrounds and means: to put an end to their drug problem.

Dorine P.,[3] one of NA's original founders in the District and known internationally among NA circles, started this courthouse meeting during the early 1980s. According to Dorine there was only one small group of NAs convening in the early 1970s; she discovered it within a little-known, dimly lit back room at the VA hospital. Now there are hundreds just in the Washington metropolitan area.

In fact, today NA, after AA and Al-Anon, is indisputably the third largest Twelve Step program going. It is estimated their ranks have swelled to half a million. The World Service Office of NA (WSO), located in Van Nuys, California, functions in almost identical fashion to AA headquarters in New York City, publishing literature, sending out "starter packets," coordinating service work, and networking for the good of the Fellowship. As of 1992, NA could be found throughout the United States, in many Canadian cities, and in over fifty-three other countries. NA published its Basic Text, or "Blue Book" (*Narcotics Anonymous*), in 1983. The companion volume, like AA's "Twelve and Twelve," entitled *It Works: How and Why,* was published in 1993. Like the Twelve and Twelve, it takes each of the Twelve Steps and Traditions, examines them in detail, and provides practical suggestions as to how they may be used in recovery. These are the two "must-read" books for the NA member.

NA patterns itself after AA in terms of the Twelve Steps and Twelve Traditions but there are major and observable differences between them (see chapter 5). This is as it should be. Most addicts, especially early in recovery, view themselves as "terminally unique." The greater variety of Twelve Step programs available on the menu simply narrows the search for the right match. NA's Twelve Steps are identical to AA's except for two noteworthy differences: (1) the word *addiction* is substituted for *alcohol* in the First Step, and (2) NA uses the word *We* in all but the Twelfth Step, whereas AA uses *We* only in the First Step.

NA began in southern California (Sun Valley) in 1953. A group of AAs, addicted to both alcohol and other drugs, sensed something missing in their AA meetings: the focus was just on alcohol rather than on addiction in general. NA takes great pride in their philosophy on addiction and recovery as expressed in their First Step: "We admitted that we were powerless over our *addiction* [italics mine], that our lives had become unmanageable." The key word is *addiction,* since NA prefers not to focus on any one particular substance. NA members believe that addiction, not the drug, is the problem for many of them.

---

3. Dorine P. works as a U.S. Probation Officer Assistant for the U.S. District Court in Washington, D.C.

As yet, NA has no formal written history. In fact, NA's legacy is that of AA's until 1953. Though they have no legendary heroes like Bill W. or Dr. Bob, members of NA make no apology for this and have no regrets. They simply respect the importance of such early AA experiences and traditions.

Correcting Misconceptions: A Quick Review

Active AA members often remind themselves of a guiding principle captured by the phrases "First things first" and "Don't pick up the first drink; it's the first one that gets you drunk." Newcomers begin to learn a new priority system. They learn to first "think the drink through." We too must be willing to let go of our misconceptions and distorted thinking about AA and most other Twelve Step groups. What follows is clarification of some of the more damaging misconceptions we have about Twelve Step programs. Some have already been mentioned, but they are important to reemphasize.

AA is NOT a religious program. It is, however, a spiritual process, a spiritual program of self-help. Do not succumb to uninformed offender assertions about the religious nature of the Fellowship. In reality, agnostics, atheists, and true believers are all welcome. Unlike religious movements, sects, or denominations, AA holds absolutely no preconception of or demand for a belief in God.

AA does NOT look disfavorably upon court referrals. AA has little regard for how the newcomer arrives. You will often hear AAs say, "Nobody walks through the door without a footprint on his or her back." Still, there are some meetings, usually smaller or located in less populous areas, where there will be resistance to the signing of court slips. Each AA group is autonomous and perfectly within its right to resist the formal signing of slips if it wishes. Because there are just as many groups very much unopposed, a person should have no difficulty finding a substitute meeting.

AA does NOT just work for the voluntary client. Yes, AA is a program of "attraction and not promotion," but do not confuse this tradition with our obligation to make mandatory referrals. We do not revoke a person's probation or parole solely on the basis of failure to attend Twelve Step meetings. We do encourage the positive and discretionary use of our court- or parole-sanctioned authority to assist in getting the offender to self-help group resources within a community. Individual jurisdictions will vary as to administrative options available for noncompliance, if any.

AA will NOT force offenders not to drink. It may ruin their drinking, but there will be no outright admonitions. Attend a few meetings and listen to the numbers of people talking about how their first experiences were the result of compulsory court sentences, or the "higher power dressed in a black robe." Feel their gratitude.

> **Note:** To those who have legal concerns about whether or not mandatory self-help group attendance violates the Establishment Clause of the First Amendment to the U.S. Constitution: In June 1994, U.S. District Judge Gary L. Taylor of the Central District of California (*O'Conner* vs. *State of California*) ruled in favor of the state's DUI education and treatment programs that routinely refer offenders to AA and other self-help groups. Significant to this ruling was that the element of personal choice remained intact. Offenders were mandated to attend self-help group meetings, and AA was the recommended vehicle for satisfaction of this condition; however, they were not prevented from using alternative secular programs, such as Rational Recovery (RR).

AA is NOT only for the "low bottom" drunk. As stated earlier, AA is often as widely misunderstood as the disease of addiction itself. But AA members are really your neighbors, your co-workers, and your leaders, not skid-row losers. You may doubt some offenders' suitability for AA, perhaps because you do not feel they fit your stereotype for active alcoholism. Refer them anyway. It could be the best "mistake" they ever experienced. Remember, it is not how much or when people drink that makes them alcoholic. It is what happens to them when they do drink (or, in the case of illegal drug use, when they do use while on supervision).

AA is NOT secretive or exclusive. This is a serious misconception, because it allows us all to make excuses for not attending AA meetings and learning as much as possible about the Fellowship. It may also inhibit us from referring "potential" alcoholics or addicts. AA has exploded in recent years, and there are a variety of "open" meetings. Visit them. Meet members of the program. Listen to their stories, ask questions, and begin to feel the process in action.

AA is NOT a quick fix. It is a lengthy and often lifetime process of personal transformation. "Old-timers" in AA will say to the newcomer, "Sobriety is a process and not an event." The principles of AA eventually become a way of life for many. They might add, "The same person will drink again; all I have to do to keep from drinking is change everything about me." Initially there is emphasis only on not drinking one day at a time. Then the focus shifts toward learning how to achieve sobriety in the sense of balance and serenity. This means changing thinking patterns, behaviors, and lifestyles.

AA is NOT treatment. Avoid the mistake of confusing AA with treatment. AA is not a class from which one is expected to graduate. Sustained abstinence from alcohol is the actual treatment, along with other professional interventions such as group or individual counseling. AA is an ongoing and entirely nonprofessional self-help group process. It is not therapy and should not compete with therapy or counseling; yet, it should *always* complement any professional treatment referral.

CHAPTER 4

Step by Step:
An Inside View of the Twelve Steps

Introduction

It has been said that people recover or stay sick depending on how well they comprehend and practice, or "work," the principles contained within the Twelve Steps. The Steps are "suggested." No one *must* do them; no one peers over your shoulder to take notes—not even sponsors, although some may be more orthodox about Step work than others. Father Martin, a pioneer in the field of recovery from alcoholism, once said, "I believe the founders of AA suggested that we use the Twelve Steps in the same way that a parachute instructor suggests that we use a parachute when we jump out of an airplane. We don't have to take the suggestion, but there are definite consequences if we don't."

Optimally, we should strive for a comfortable understanding and well-grounded "feel" for each of the Steps. We cannot expect to insist on offender involvement in the program unless we, as referring agents, are privy to a major part of the offender's reality. We cannot encourage offenders to talk about their experiences with the Steps unless we have a knowledge basis of our own; unless we too are Twelve Step-literate. We certainly cannot take advantage of the most practical way to determine whether or not someone is attending meetings (without using court slips) unless we have more than just a superficial acquaintance with the Steps. We merely *suggest* you not do the one without the other.

Our discussion of the Twelve Steps and what AA members often talk about within their meetings relative to those Steps is drawn from a combination of personal visits; a few AA friendships; two of AA's most widely read publications—the books *Alcoholics Anonymous,* known as the "Big Book," and *Twelve Steps and Twelve Traditions,* known as the "Twelve and Twelve"; and finally, Terence Gorski's *Understanding the Twelve Steps.* Although we focus exclusively on AA in the context of this discussion, our comments and interpretation are just as valid for persons working other Twelve Step programs (such as NA or CA).

Be mindful that the discussion material within each Step is selective. We tried to highlight common concerns and issues, but it is by no means exhaustive. The "Step Work Pointers" section following each Step is meant to be used as a summary or quick review of practical points involved in working the foregoing Step. One final caveat before we begin: Learning about the Steps is only the beginning. There can be no better substitute than actual visits to the meetings themselves.

STEP WORK POINTERS
(General)

- "Step work" or "Working the Steps," simply means making the best effort, on a consistent basis, to apply the basic principles intrinsic to each Step in all areas of one's life. Step work is the suggested practical way to achieve and sustain one's sobriety. Perhaps this crude formula captures it best: Step Work + Meetings = Long-Term Sobriety.

- The Steps are numbered sequentially for a reason; most in recovery suggest working them in order.

- Not finishing one Step before going on to the next can be dangerous. This is called "two-stepping." It refers to the act of completing the First Step but then skipping to others up the ladder, potentially missing vital building blocks of recovery.

- The Steps are meant to be worked more than once. Most active AA members view their practice of the Twelve Steps as a lifelong process. Starting all over again, well into sobriety, is not at all uncommon; many will learn something entirely new each time they work them through.

- There is no timetable for working the Steps. One does not do a Step a week and "graduate" at the end of twelve weeks. Someone with a solid four years of recovery might identify oneself as "sitting on Step Four," not having yet completed the personal inventory. This may be okay for this person (and, in all likelihood, a mere technicality or excessively rigid identification). In reality, the person who has been around a while and has been actively attending meetings has probably worked beyond Step Four.

The Foundation Steps (1–3)

Step One: Or, I Can't Stop Alone

> *We admitted we were powerless over alcohol—that our lives had become unmanageable.*

This is the foundation Step of true recovery: admitting defeat, and thereby positioning oneself for outside help. The people who take this Step accept that they are no longer able to control their addiction and that their efforts to do so have made it impossible to manage their lives. AAs assert that this is the only Step requiring 100 percent perfection. It also cuts to the very core of an alcoholic's need to keep in mind that AA is a "no-drinking program." There will be talk of "surrendering to win" and learning to stay away from a drink "one day at a time." This becomes a daily first Step, which must be completed *perfectly.*

In meetings, a person will hear others share their stories. They will talk about how they came to admit their life-threatening condition, whether it be through the court system, an angry spouse, or an intolerant employer. Focus is generally on past denial issues, arrogant attitudes, or persistent refusals to openly admit the existence of a problem despite an underlying sense that their relationship to alcohol was unique. We have found it very encouraging to visit "open" meetings and witness, over and over again, the positive leverage brought about by an informed probation officer who insists that his or her offender go to "those meetings."

Suggesting that an offender examine his or her relationship to alcohol and other drugs within the context of this First Step can be very helpful. Step One is about making the vital connection between the use of alcohol or drugs and the problems one is experiencing in one's life. Using, despite adverse consequences is the hallmark of addictive disease. An attempt to concretize the powerlessness component of this First Step is critical. Treatment programs often ask their patients to "write out" their First Step, which simply means to tell their story.

Further on in recovery (months, perhaps years), many people in the program make reference to powerlessness over "people, places, and things" in a more general sense, as the Step takes on a different and less literal meaning for them. A symbolic first step is taken when an individual chooses to say, "My name is Bob and I am an alcoholic" or "My name is Tom and I am powerless over drugs and alcohol."

STEP WORK POINTERS

- In completing this Step a person must admit four things:
  - That alcohol or drug use has caused major problems
  - That one is powerless to control one's drug/alcohol use
  - That life has become unmanageable as a result of using
  - That one remains powerless to manage life if use continues

- It is the drinking or drugging that causes the addict's problems, not external events or circumstances like angry spouses, troublesome employers, bad traffic jams, or uncooperative and ignorant people.

- Remember: Admitting "powerlessness" over alcohol or drugs does not mean that addicts have no power over other significant aspects of their life. It simply means, for most addicts anyway, that once the drug or alcohol is ingested, they can no longer, with 100 percent accuracy, predict the outcome of their use or consequent behavior.

Step Two: Or, We Can Stop Together

Came to believe that a Power greater than ourselves could restore us to sanity.

It is here for the first time that the AA newcomer faces the suggested use of a "Higher Power" (HP) to help remove the deadly compulsion to drink. HP is an entirely personal concept; for some it is the AA group or an understanding sponsor; *it is anything but individual willpower.* The word *sanity,* in this context, refers to soundness of mind, or not continuing to drink or drug in the face of dangerous signs of addiction. Sheer personal resolve against a drink gets cast aside for something more powerful and outside the self. Willpower and a personal resolve to get better are necessary for motivating a person to attend meetings, but they should not be confused with the disastrous results willpower has yielded in the area of trying to keep oneself from drinking.

The First Step is one of admitting the problem, of admitting, "I can't handle it on my own." The Second Step addresses acceptance and the hope of a better and sober life yet to come *if* one is willing to let somebody else help. People in AA talk about "coming to believe" that there might really be a life beyond alcohol, but they must first resign from the debating society and stick with the winners in the Fellowship.

STEP WORK POINTERS

- Do not be reluctant to talk with newcoming offenders about what it means to find a Higher Power or to point out that relying on themselves this far in life has obviously not shown prodigious results.
- Encourage offenders to consider turning to the experts for their Higher Power: the Twelve Step group itself.
- Working and/or completing this Step involves two primary tasks:
  - Coming to accept that a person is suffering from "addiction-induced insanity," which creates the obsession and compulsion to use
  - Coming to accept that this insanity can only be removed with outside help

Step Three: Or, Making a Commitment to the Program

Made a decision to turn our will and our lives over to the care of God as we understood Him.

This Step is about the willingness to "let go and let God." By making this decision, the newcomer makes a commitment to stick with the program, to see it out, and to walk through life's tribulations without resorting to alcohol or drugs. Paradoxical and difficult for the strong-willed, this Step is asking for surrender to the God of one's understanding (or to one's Higher Power, whether it be the group, a sponsor, or AA as a whole) as means of achieving an independence of spirit. Colloquially, it means to "turn it over"; that is, whatever the problem is, let go and allow your HP to guide and direct. Individual ideas about faith are frequently discussed. Fears concerning what will become of individuality and self-determination once "turned over" are shared. "Self-centered fear" is the phrase used to describe a common alcoholic personality trait: the fear of losing something I have and not getting something I demand.

It is not unusual for a person to work the first three Steps for months and years. Remember, this is a "process and not an event." An individual may need to experience the pains of "white-knuckle" sobriety before he or she is willing to accept a future payoff in making the decision. Some AAs believe that this Step, once taken, is a closed book. Others think it is repeatedly practiced over the course of their lives. It is not at all unusual for a person with a substantial number of years in sobriety to reaffirm his or her need to practice Step Three. Underlying the Third Step is the notion that *abstinence alone is not recovery* and that spiritual action (even if only in the form of "praying with your feet," or attending meetings regularly) is necessary for sustained growth and sobriety.

STEP WORK POINTERS

- We must help offenders not get mired in an ill-defined religious defensiveness or struggle over the real meaning of this Step. Break it down to its simplest form: Should they stay or should they go? Should they stay with the program, "turn over" their drinking or drugging problem to the group, and move on to Step Four? Or should they dismiss it all over superficial semantics?

- Do not misinterpret the word *care;* note that it says the *care* of God *as we understood Him,* not the *control.*

- The bottom line for working this Step is accepting help from an outside source, being willing to start relying on others for help, listening to suggestions from others in the Fellowship, and following simple directions. It means an end to complete self-reliance and the beginning of faith.

- Working this Step also means the following:
  - Using professional help for problems other than addiction
  - Using spiritual principles to help guide other aspects of one's life
  - Starting to recognize when one's own ideas start to conflict with those of the program
  - Making the recovery experience a real part of one's daily living; e.g., spending as much time in meetings during the first year as one used to spend in a bar or exercising another drug habit

- Many "beginner's meetings" focus only on Steps 1–3. Newcomers can often pick up a good sense of the program by attending these meetings. Many old-timers return to them for the feeling of gratitude it gives them, remembering "from whence they came."

Steps of Reflection (4–6)

Step Four: Or, Taking an Honest Look at Myself

Made a searching and fearless moral inventory of ourselves.

The willingness to venture into this Step assumes the Third Step has been taken. Only by having some faith in the program (and a commitment to see it through), or a Higher Power, will a person possess enough humility to start the suggested self-examination process. This time it will be with pen and paper in hand as the AA member completes a written inventory of personal assets and liabilities (also called "shortcomings" or "character defects") that have gotten in the way of comfortable living. Designed to address the emotional pains, secrets, fears, and embarrassments of the past (including the pre-drinking years), this Step signifies an important commitment to move on in the program.

Practically speaking, there are many different methods for completing the Fourth Step or enhancing one's awareness of *Self in* sobriety. The Big Book encourages a detailed analysis of one's resentments and how relationships with people or institutions have affected self-esteem, sexuality, pride, security, and status. The Big Book (p. 65) lays out definite examples as follows:

I'm resentful at	The cause	Affects my
Mr. Brown	His attention to my wife Told my wife of my mistress	Sex relations Self-esteem (fear)
My employer	Unreasonable—Unjust— Overbearing—	Self-esteem (fear)

Some AA sponsors simply suggest that people take a piece of paper and pencil, write out the worst thing they ever did in their life, "the one thing they were going to the grave with," and then turn the page over and start writing about themselves, especially about their relationships with others. They should include their unreasonable demands for "sex, security, and status." Much of the writing will wind up in their "drunk-a-log" or story; but the people who are really serious about delving deep will recognize "character defects" and personality flaws that existed well before they first picked up a drink or drug.

By now, it should be obvious why the Fourth Step is a stumbling block for many newcomers and is best accompanied by a good sponsor relationship. It is difficult to find the requisite honesty, especially when viewed in the context of the following Step and the need to actually share one's findings with another. Many AAs choose to do several Fourth Steps over the course of their sobriety; they find the capacity to look deeper grows as they move further in time from their last drink or drug.

STEP FOUR

STEP WORK POINTERS

- Addiction is a multifaceted disease with a complex variety of components or antecedents, including the emotional, behavioral, and spiritual. Now that the drug or alcohol has been removed, the next Step seems logical: take a good long look at what remains. What is there to work with, positive and negative, now that the addict is straight or drug-free?

- Recovery demands change. According to the wisdom of AA, it is simple: "The same person will drink or use again." Or, as put to the naive newcomer who inquires what he or she must do to get clean and sober and stay that way, "All you have to do is change everything about yourself."

- How do you spot a person supposedly in recovery who has not completed his or her Fourth Step? Look for a "dry drunk"; a person with many resentments; a person who remains irritable, excessively critical, miserable, and difficult to live with, even though he or she is drug free.

- Should you not have other corroborative verification on hand, working on or having completed a Fourth Step is one of the most reliable indicators that a person is serious about his or her program involvement.

- Most rehabilitative programs require their patients to complete a Fourth Step inventory prior to discharge.

- There are hundreds of Fourth Step guides available on the market or from established treatment centers. Some have a series of questions, quite detailed and exhaustive, that require addicts to go back through their life and examine themselves in terms of early family relationships, sexuality, and friendships. Some spend weeks and months preparing this document for sharing with their sponsor or spiritual advisor. For many, it is a major event to finally attend a meeting and say they have completed their Fourth Step!

- Anger and resentment are two of the most frequently talked-about emotions in all Twelve Step meetings. This should not be surprising as you reflect on a caseload of addicted offenders, particularly those fortunate enough to come to terms with this emotional facet of their "dis-ease."

Step Five: Or, Sharing the Human Connection

Admitted to God, to ourselves, and to another human being the exact nature of our wrongs.

You hear in meetings how a person finally felt like part of the program once he or she completed this Step. After finding the strength or being cajoled (some sponsors push to move on *immediately* after the Fourth) to do the Fifth, most people feel a comforting sense of relief. Doing the Fifth Step is a significant milestone within the recovering community. It involves a process of breaking down barriers ("peeling away layers of the onion"), discovering various twists on "self-centered fear," continuing the practice of rigorous honesty, and working on sharing the human connection or person-to-person trust.

Most AA groups recommend that newcomers share their Fifth Step with a sponsor. Some opt for a spiritual advisor or priest. Many men and women, working with same-sex sponsors, as recommended, stumble on the beginning of a friendship characterized by nonsexual intimacy, honesty, and true compassion. Some talk about the end of isolation as they realize they are no longer alone with their secrets. Sponsors share their negative experiences and fears as well, helping solidify the human connectedness. They say that "you are only as sick as your secrets"; and with most recovering addicts, there are numerous guilt-ridden emotions and incidents of the past which, if not openly admitted and talked about, could interfere with comfortable sobriety.

Step Five is rarely "two-stepped" or practiced out of order; it is far more often ignored or consciously avoided. This is because it takes faith and an equally strong assurance that what you have to share will be compassionately understood and kept confidential. To some, it means taking a leap of faith; for the first time they are truly relying on something, somebody else outside of themselves to help guide their life. Working through the Fifth Step puts an end to years of isolation and lays the groundwork for the development of healthy personal relationships.

STEP WORK POINTERS

- One of the secondary gains to this Step comes with the sponsor's greater understanding of the sponsee. If practiced well, the sponsor will intuitively know how to use this new information (some of it very delicately, of course) in a way that will strengthen the sponsee's sobriety.

- Any offender who talks openly about having either thought about completing or completed a Fifth Step can usually be trusted to have made a sincere commitment to the recovery process. It is not a Step that one takes on lightly, or alone, for obvious reasons.

- Typically, the sponsor and sponsee agree upon an evening. An appointment is made, and the sponsor and sponsee get together. The newcomer brings his or her written Fourth Step. They talk, sometimes for hours, sometimes much shorter. Each circumstance is very different.

- We must be quick to remind offenders that it is self-defeating to keep the contents of a Fourth Step secret and that the majority of relapsers admit they "never got around to the Fifth."

- Encourage offenders who are active in the program, those who have taken the Fifth Step, to listen to and accept the advice and direction from the person in whom they have confided.

- Being on the listening or receiving end of a Fifth Step is described in meetings as a very powerful experience. Sponsors openly express their gratitude that they were given the sobriety to "pass it on" or to share their "experience, strength, and hope."

- Know that much of what transpires in traditional therapy groups is really a professional Fifth Step exercise.

Step Six: Or, Getting Ready to Move on in Sobriety

Were entirely ready to have God remove all these defects of character.

In the preceding two Steps the person began to identify important character traits or defects that stood in the way of continued growth, spiritual development, and, ultimately, serenity. Now that the facts and feelings of one's personality (the "real me") are accepted, an authentic change process is initiated. A person slowly (sometimes it takes years) begins to understand and accept the fact that although alcohol may no longer be an issue, most of the normal day-to-day living problems remain as strong as ever. This Step stresses the mental and spiritual preparation necessary to achieve the willingness to move on and work *toward character improvement.* Often a person will be driven to work this Step following a "dry drunk" or "emotional bender." Coming to the realization that drinking behavior is but a part of the whole problem is at the heart of this Step. Such a realization can be very disconcerting: Why did I get sober in the first place . . . for what? To feel this lousy, to still do these insensitive things?

On first reading, this Step appears "easy," or at least passive, in orientation. In reality it demands a great deal of work, a sizable amount of courage, and the *willingness* to change negative behavior, destructive thinking patterns, and self-defeating attitudes . . . *in sobriety.*

STEP SIX

STEP WORK POINTERS

- The AA publication entitled *Twelve Steps and Twelve Traditions,* known as the "Twelve and Twelve," refers to this Step as the one that separates the "men from the boys" (or the girls from the women). It is spiritually demanding.
- Working Step Six is not a one-shot proposition. In fact, people work at it throughout their lives; they remain committed to the

personal change or growth process and periodically encounter character defects, habits, or behavior that gets in the way of their peacefulness or serenity.

- The biggest stumbling block to this Step is having to admit that *even in sobriety* one will face character defects that often evolve into self-defeating behaviors with problematic consequences, including potential for relapse.

Steps of Reconciliation (7–9)

Step Seven: Or, Asking for Help Again

Humbly asked Him to remove our shortcomings.

Just as the AA member solicited the help of a Higher Power in removing the compulsion to drink (Steps 1–3), he or she may now seek spiritual guidance to combat the character flaws, still present in sobriety, that stand in the way of serenity. Emotional pain may inevitably be the only real motivator. For example, one person may choose to work on a self-destructive tendency to control and manage the lives of others. Another may decide that procrastination or spending money is distracting him or her from growth.

By praying to a Higher Power, talking to others in the Fellowship, attending meetings, and continually asking for help, AAs face the power of the program that extends beyond simple abstinence. AAs have been known to say "our character defects are removed in the order in which they are killing us." The addiction to substance is first. It will be followed by other, less immediately fatal, impediments to sober (i.e., balanced or reasonable) living.

STEP SEVEN

STEP WORK POINTERS

- Steps Six and Seven are very spiritual in nature. They both demand a comfortable acceptance of a Higher Power.
- People working this Step must be reminded that they are not all-powerful, that they alone cannot remove these stubborn character traits or destructive habits in sobriety. Help must come from without.

- Honestly working this Step suggests that the person must do the following:
  - Recognize the value of humility and that an overreliance on self and isolation from others—and their HP—has created serious problems in and out of recovery
  - Understand that one cannot live comfortably by one's own individual strength and intelligence alone, that faith must develop so others outside of oneself (people, HP, etc.) may be relied upon as well
  - Accept the challenge to work on character building, to continually examine one's goals in life, and to work toward greater spiritual values
- Self-centered fear, defined as "primarily fear that we would lose something we already possessed or would fail to get something we demanded," is a frequently used phrase in the context of the Seventh Step. People talk about self-centered fear as being the real culprit behind most defects of character.

Step Eight: Or, Identifying the Victims

Made a list of all persons we had harmed, and became willing to make amends to them all.

Similar to the Fourth Step in terms of reflection, this Step focuses exclusively on personal relationships. Interpersonal relationships have usually presented significant problems: there are hurt and damaged spouses, lovers, employers, crime victims, and institutions to whom amends may be owed. By forgiving the harms done by others and discussing the list with a sponsor, a person becomes willing to entertain the action required of the next Step.

STEP EIGHT

STEP WORK POINTERS

- A person who works this Step takes pen to paper and makes a list, discusses it with his or her sponsor, and then is usually counseled to hold off for a time before moving on and making the actual amends.

- The best place to find out who belongs on the list is to go back to the Fourth Step inventory. Doing the Eighth Step is a Fourth Step review and is suitable for those who failed at thoroughness on their earlier inventory.

- Forgiveness is the spiritual goal as well as stumbling block to the completion of this Step. Many alcoholics and addicts have been victims themselves (often by their own family). Not letting go of these resentments typically creates a formidable barrier to finding the willingness to make the amends.

Step Nine: Or, Into Action on the Amends

Made direct amends to such people wherever possible, except when to do so would injure them or others.

Making an effort to clear the "wreckage of the past" is the hallmark of this Step. Not simply an apology, but actual change becomes a key concept as program members try to approach (or not approach, as the case may be) the people or institutions listed on their Eighth Step. "Making amends" could mean a letter to an old girlfriend, paying more attention to one's family, or making direct restitution to an injured employer. It is often confused with a simple apology, but it really connotes serious behavioral change. A newcomer who does little more than not drink one day at a time is making an important contribution to this Step.

Step Nine is discussed in chapter 6 of the Big Book of AA. One of the most commonly read and talked about sections of this chapter, entitled "Into Action," contains the "Promises." The early members of AA assured their readers that these Promises would come true for *anyone* willing to work Steps One through Nine. There are twelve of them as quoted below:

The Promises

If we are painstaking about this phase of our development, we will be amazed before we are half way through. We are going to know a new freedom and a new happiness. We will not regret the past nor wish to shut the door on it. We will comprehend the word serenity and we will know peace. No matter how far down the scale we have gone, we will see how our experience can benefit others. That feeling of uselessness and self-pity will disappear. We will lose interest in selfish things and gain interest in our fellows. Self-seeking will slip away. Our whole attitude and outlook upon life will change. Fear of people and economic insecurity will leave us. We will intuitively know how to handle situations which used to baffle us. We will suddenly realize that God is doing for us what we could not do for ourselves.

STEP WORK POINTERS

- More often than not, sponsors find themselves cautioning restraint. One frequently hears in meetings about the overzealous and premature "apology" that resulted in a humiliating rebuff . . . and excuse for relapse.

- Sometimes the best possible amend is for the addict or alcoholic to simply stay out of a person's life altogether (usually an estranged spouse, sibling, or family member) and continue his or her commitment to the recovery process.

- Some people in the program work this Step by acknowledging that they owe "amends" to themselves for years of damage and self-inflicted pain. They seek new ways of treating themselves to good things, of reinforcing the progress they have made thus far in their sobriety.

- Experienced program members stress the importance of working with a sponsor to develop a plan for making amends to people and institutions, as the case may be, and above all, approaching it with "an attitude of quiet sincerity."

The Maintenance Steps (10–12)

Step Ten: Or, Self-Examination While "Clean"

Continued to take personal inventory and when we were wrong promptly admitted it.

This is the first of the "maintenance Steps." Designed to be used as a tool for maintaining sobriety, Step Ten becomes a stabilizing influence, a barometer of a person's emotional balance at any particular moment in time. A quick on-the-spot inventory could reveal a dangerous thought pattern ("stinking thinking"), an old character defect popping up again, or the need to simply be quiet and not respond to an angry thought or emotion. Many choose to put an end to their day by doing a Tenth Step before bed. Not having taken a drink that day will often stand at the head of the list.

STEP TEN

STEP WORK POINTERS

- For many—and this is perfectly acceptable—working this Step rarely goes beyond immediate anger management, or learning how to "count to ten" before reacting to something someone said or did.

- Others will work on close examination of their remaining character defects like selfishness, dishonesty, resentments, and fear. "How are these negative attributes continuing to affect the relationships I have with others, with myself, and with my Higher Power?"

- In AA meetings on this Step, participants will talk about the gains they have made in controlling their temper, admitting mistakes to spouses, and not flying off the handle.

- This is a Step that demands attention every day, sometimes several times a day, because it involves a continuous self-reflection process that ends up with a balance sheet as to how well or how poorly someone lived up to the principles of the program that day.

- The Tenth Step means putting a stop to taking other people's inventories; learning how to humbly examine one's own short-comings; and knowing that if one stops growing and changing, he or she will be that much more prone to relapse. Abstinence alone is not recovery.

Step Eleven: Or, Learning to Grow through Meditation

Sought through prayer and meditation to improve our conscious contact with God as we understood Him, praying only for knowledge of His will for us and the power to carry that out.

Recovering alcoholics or other addicts, comfortable with their program and intent upon further growth, will talk openly of their consistent use of this Step.

Many old-timers will credit their entire sobriety, in the less literal sense, to working extremely hard on the development of a close relationship with their Higher Power. Learning meditation skills for self-reflection also becomes a central component of their maintenance work.

STEP ELEVEN

STEP WORK POINTERS

- In some areas of the country, there are Eleventh Step "retreats" (spiritually oriented weekends) or AA meetings that focus exclusively on the Eleventh Step.

- Meetings on the Eleventh Step will always include people talking about various ways they pray (an "appeal" to God or HP), or meditate ("listening" for the response), and how they try very hard to work on the development of a "personal relationship" to the God of their understanding.

- Agnostics talk in meetings about their struggle with spirituality, how difficult it is for them to change years of disbelief, and what a challenge it is to discipline themselves to pray or "act as if" there may indeed be a God, even despite the evidence in their lives to the contrary.

- By working this Step people come to acknowledge that miraculous changes have come about since their original commitment to work the Steps. Their willpower was not enough to make them stop drinking; most of the change occurred when they finally surrendered and listened to "God speak through others."

- Morning meditation is a trademark program activity for someone serious about the Eleventh Step.

- Newcomers often need counseling and clarification on their prayer methodology, given their tendency to ask for or pray for specifics like material things or new relationships.

Step Twelve: Or, Beginning to Help Others

Having had a spiritual awakening as the result of these steps, we tried to carry this message to alcoholics, and to practice these principles in all our affairs.

This Step is all about the "joy of living." In meetings, members talk about love that has no price tag, service work for AA, passing the message on to other suffering alcoholics, sponsorship, spiritual growth, applying these principles of living to their daily affairs, and having gratitude for blessings received.

"Spiritual awakening" means different things to different people. For most active program members, it simply suggests they have been around long enough to *actively* work the preceding Eleven Steps, attend plenty of meetings, and undergo such profound change (biological, emotional, behavioral, and spiritual) that there was only one possible consequence: *gratitude about being an alcoholic in the first place!*

STEP TWELVE

STEP WORK POINTERS

- Working this Step means a lot of different things:
  - Being able to tell all three parts of one's story (what it was like, what happened, and what it is like now)
  - Getting into "service work," such as being program chair, secretary, or coffee-maker for a group
  - Being a sponsor or answering phones at the "desk"
  - Doing traditional Twelfth Step work, or being called upon to visit someone (usually at home) and either take that person to his or her first meeting or perhaps the hospital, as the case may be
- Although this contradicts the earlier caveat about working the Steps in numerical order, people are encouraged to embrace the Twelfth Step prior to formal completion of the preceding Steps. "Two-stepping," or going from Step One to Step Twelve and, thereby, taking advantage of a newcomer's vulnerability (often of the opposite sex) is not looked upon favorably. Launching into Step Nine before doing the Fourth Step is not recommended either. However, taking the Steps in order is not totally sacrosanct. The more existential point

of view suggests that in the process of working any one Step, some facet of all the others is touched.

- People who work this Step continue to attend meetings and participate in the sharing of their "experience, strength, and hope," even though they have achieved stable sobriety and may not need to go to meetings for themselves. They are likely to say the easiest thing they do each day is not take a drink or a drug—the tough part is learning how to live a balanced and purposeful life by practicing Twelve Step principles in all their affairs.

CHAPTER 5

Working the Program:
Practical Supervision Techniques

The Hidden Message

Just try to refer anyone *anywhere* without familiarizing yourself with or having confidence in the resource. For most of us practitioners, it is unlikely to work. We become self-conscious. The offender picks up on our insecurity. We lapse into a condescending or overly authoritative tone and lose out before we even begin. In criminal justice, trust between the refer*er* and the refer*ee* is minimal at best. They know we don't trust them, that in most cases we never will. Under such conditions, the odds for successful follow-through are not promising. So our challenge is to create an educated and individually sensitive referral atmosphere.

Routinely "directing," "ordering," or "instructing" an offender to start attending AA, NA, or some other Twelve Step group initially translates to an offender as *That person is telling me I am weak, needy, and helpless.* To many offenders the very idea of having to go to "those meetings" is worse than having a record in the first place. This is the pejorative undercurrent or hidden message that many offenders find in a perfunctory Twelve Step referral. We become wedded to such routine because many of us are either too busy or too preoccupied.

The making of a Twelve Step program referral is a professional skill, an art of sorts that demands finding the right referral source and a willingness to listen and ask questions in the process. It is not easy and, therefore, should not be matter-of-fact. Most offenders will be resistant and uninformed. Many others will be manipulative and downright arrogant. Finding a way to be simultaneously firm, patient, understanding, and informative comes only with knowledge and practice.

Doing *Our* Homework

As pointed out earlier, AA and NA are anonymous programs. However, they are not secret or exclusive. Without question the most effective and professionally responsible way to improve our knowledge of and feel for the Twelve Step programs is to attend meetings ourselves. If you do nothing else, do this; it is that critically significant. The Twelve Step programs have expanded dramatically in recent years, and there are a variety of "open" meetings that encourage visitation by community professionals. Ideally, we will have strong management support for this; administrators and supervisors should authorize compensatory time, administrative leave, or other ways of assuring proper exposure.

Going to only one or two AA meetings is not recommended. Not only is there a risk of missing out on the subtle experiential differences between Twelve Step group orientations (AA vs. NA vs. Al-Anon vs. Nar-Anon), but there is also a good chance of coming up short on an informed judgment about the Fellowship as a whole. Most newcoming offenders do just that: attend one or two meetings and make up their minds that it couldn't be for them. Do not make the same mistake; give it a fair shake over time and different meetings. We recommend "six weeks of meetings or six different meetings," as the saying goes in Al-Anon. Here is a short list of reasons why actual visitation is so important:

- *It reminds us that we do make a difference,* that our focus on "raising the bottom" and intervening in people's lives does work. Attend enough meetings, and you *will* hear ex-offenders talk about the gratitude they feel because their P.O. (or the Court, or their lawyer) "forced" them to go to AA or NA. What was initially mandated attendance has turned voluntary.

- *It deepens our understanding of addictive disease in general.* Attending meetings is about as close as many of us will get to feeling the pain, the powerlessness, and the sheer craziness of addiction. Consider the proverbial offender retort designed to distract and throw us off guard: "How can you help me if you've never been through what I've been through? How would you have any idea what those meetings are like?" By exposing ourselves to meetings we obviate such antagonistic "flip-back" queries and can then offer a more meaningful response.

- *It decreases burnout.* It is no secret that we are susceptible to burnout; those of us in criminal justice, saturated with offender pathology and negativism, need to be reminded that we do make an impact. Attending meetings serves as this reminder, for there we will encounter the "winners." We will recognize that the program does work, that recovery is possible.

- *Our public image as community corrections professionals is enhanced by attending meetings.* It shows we care and that we are open-minded. It shows the community (and, ultimately, the offenders, of course) that we are interested in addiction and what works within the recovery community.

- *Making program contacts and establishing new referral information* is another likely outcome of meeting attendance. In so doing we keep abreast of new groups, current directories, possible local sponsorship programs or activities, new clubs, and available literature.

- *We build "veracity radar" by attending meetings.* Working toward Twelve Step literacy from this experiential angle, we become more savvy in determining whether or not the offender is actually going to meetings in the first place, with or without signature "slips."

> **A Final Note:** When visiting a meeting or group, put yourself in the newcoming offender's shoes. Imagine being there for the first time. Recognize the insecurity that creeps in. Feel the impulse to run from these new people with whom you feel nothing in common. Imagine their resentment at being told to be there in the first place. And feel the potential for isolation, as you witness pockets of friends who know one another, feel comfortable with one another, and are laughing and joking together. It usually takes time and many future visits for the offender to start to get comfortable.

Types of Meetings

The multiplicity and individuality of available groups is nothing less than daunting, depending on your geographic location. There are small and intimate groups, some with only a handful of members in regular attendance. There are groups that choose to remain extra anonymous and are not listed in area directories. There are large celebratory or anniversary meetings, characterized by impressive numbers of people, traditional podiums, well-known AA or NA speakers, and palpable electricity. There are AA and NA clubs or buildings leased to groups that often have meetings around the clock and always have special "marathon" meetings during traditionally relapse-prone times, like major holidays. There are closed meetings, open meetings, open-speaker meetings, Big Book meetings, Tradition meetings, Step meetings, discussion groups, gratitude meetings, beginners' meetings, "chip" meetings, and an additional variety of special-interest-group meetings for lawyers, doctors, foreign services officers, pilots, gay men, lesbians, depressives, and others who feel they need the support of a more homogenous atmosphere for their recovery effort.

Here is a listing of typical Twelve Step meetings from which we can choose to shape the offender referral. Group or meeting formats change according to the group's needs. Groups start up, change format, close down, and move all the time. This list is not comprehensive or accurate for everywhere. Although there will be definite similarities, there are distinct geographical variations.

Open Meetings

Open meetings are open to anyone interested in attending, including the general public, other interested professionals, and, of course, community corrections staff who want to expand their experiential resource base. One very important caveat, though: Visitors and friends are expected to respect the anonymity of all people they see or meet at these meetings.

Closed Meetings

These are meetings for persons who have or think they may have a desire to stop drinking or drugging (or doing whatever the maladaptive behavior is for other Twelve Step groups). The purpose of a closed meeting is to discuss the recovery process in a way that gives individual members maximum opportunity to ask questions and express themselves more freely with other recovering alcoholics and addicts.

> **Notes:** There will be circumstances when we choose to steer an offender to one or the other kind of meeting. Closed meetings tend to be smaller. People still unsure about their identity as an addict or alcoholic are welcome in closed meetings, as long as they have a desire, genuine or otherwise, not to drink or drug that day. Generally, although one has to be very careful when making generalizations about groups that are so intrinsically autonomous and different, closed meetings are populated more by people with demonstrated clean or sober time; there may be more emphasis on living problems, working the Steps, and less on "drunk- or drug-a-log" stories.

Traditions Meetings

There are variations, but this format typically involves a group that decides to devote part of an evening or an entire meeting (either every week, a first Monday of the month, or once a quarter, after a full cycle of Step meetings) to a discussion of one or more of the Twelve Traditions. Group leaders often have substantial amounts of time in sobriety.

Discussion Meetings

Open or closed (check the local directory codes) discussion meetings are the standard meeting formats in most areas. The group's program chair will ask someone to lead the meeting each week. This person will normally "qualify" himself or herself for a few minutes—share his or her story about what it used to be like and how it is now—and then discuss a recovery topic, whether it be a specific Step (One through Twelve) or simply what tools he or she used that day to stay clean or sober. The leader will then go around the room and call on people or ask for volunteers. No one gets upset if a participant gets off topic, especially if the content has anything to do with not drinking or drugging.

Speakers Meetings

Speakers meetings are, by design, generally open to the public. They form the historically accepted open format conducive to passing on the message of sobriety. From a participant's standpoint, they are the least threatening and usually the largest. One, two, or three recovering members share their story of recovery for approximately fifteen to twenty minutes each, sometimes followed by a discussion open to all.

The message is one of hope as alcoholics or other addicts recount the progression of their disease, what they were like during their denial, when and how they bottomed out, and what happened to motivate them to seek a different life. Most will also describe what it has been like *since* coming to the program—what the Steps have done for them and what being clean and sober is like today.

Ideally, newcomers "identify in" or hear parts of their own experience as they push beyond the denial. Old-timers and others already comfortable with their recovery feel gratitude as they "keep green" and remember what it was like for them early on.

> **Notes:** It is seductively easy to hide in speakers meetings. There is no pressure to speak, to take part in the meeting, or to contribute. In many, just because of size alone, group members are not likely to approach newcomers afterwards and welcome them. A sensitive person could walk away with an "attitude" about this. However, for someone reluctant to say the dreaded words "I'm John and I'm an alcoholic [or addict]," this could be the place to start. One final caveat: An offender who is genuinely involved in a Twelve Step program will normally attend more "closed" (Step or discussion) meetings than speakers meetings.

Step Meetings

Most often "closed," the Step meeting runs a format similar to that of the discussion group with but one exception: the topic is always one of the Twelve Steps. The classic model runs on a quarterly basis, twelve weeks at a time, with each week devoted to a certain Step. Sometimes at the end of a cycle, a Traditions meeting will be held before beginning again with Step One.

The leader will talk for ten to twenty minutes about either that particular Step, his or her story and how it might relate to that Step, or both, before opening it up to the rest of the group for discussion. Members try to stay focused on the Step and how it relates to their program. Or one can certainly "pass" and not say anything.

> **Notes:** If a variety of meeting formats are available, encourage attendance at closed Step meetings. Generally, and we say this with significant caution given the autonomous nature of each area and its groups of meetings, Step meetings are typically smaller, more intensely focused on how to stay sober with the Steps, and attended by persons with lengthier periods of sobriety or clean time. Step meetings tend to have fewer "slip signers" and involuntary participants. Those who are sincere in their ambivalence about their drinking or drugging and are perhaps very worried about anonymity should be referred to this format. Going to a speakers meeting limits the field of possible identification options to 1, 2, or 3 (the primary speakers) as opposed to several more. Feelings, attitudes, and honest fears are more likely to come out in closed meetings, within either the Step or discussion format.

Big Book or Text-Study Meetings

A leader will make a few opening comments and then read segments from either *Alcoholics Anonymous* (the "Big Book") or *Narcotics Anonymous* (the "Blue Book"). After a paragraph or two and perhaps a personal comment related to the material, the book is passed to the next person for continued reading and further comment, if he or she chooses. For someone interested in the totality of the Twelve Step experience, with a special emphasis on history, this is the meeting to attend.

Beginner's Meetings

Most beginner's meetings are open and focus on discussion of the first three Steps. Typically, there is less overall sobriety (i.e., chronologically) within these rooms compared to closed Step meetings. Some members like to intersperse their meeting regimen with beginner's meetings, both to keep their memories fresh as to what it was like for them and because they find it easier to find potential sponsees to whom they can "carry the message."

Notes: Beginner's meetings tend to be more tolerant of "slip-signers" and referrals from community corrections. For a person struggling with the first three Steps, the recovery program's foundation, this is an excellent place to begin. For someone with "time in" who needs to start practicing the Twelfth step, this is where to go. And for an individual who is either unsure or in denial, this is also a suitable format.

Chip Meetings

These are groups, either closed or open, and Step-, discussion-, or speaker-oriented, that hand out medallions ("chips"), key rings (NA, primarily), and other mementos or souvenirs attesting to various lengths of sobriety or clean time. People are asked if they want to celebrate one, three, six, or nine months and then multiples of one year on. If it happens to be someone's clean and sober anniversary date, or if the date has already passed, he or she may opt to stand and be acknowledged. After these yearly multiples, the *most important person in the room* will be recognized if he or she so chooses: the person who either has twenty-four hours of clean and sober time or the *desire* to stay clean and sober that day.

Note: Chips and medallions can be purchased by contacting either Hazelden Educational Materials (1-800-328-9000) or each of the respective national headquarters for AA and NA (see appendix A). Take note that the color codes for NA key chains, seemingly used with more frequency than medallions (at least in the Washington, D.C., area) are as follows:

24 hour or Welcome = White
30 days = Orange
60 days = Green
90 days = Red
6 months = Blue
9 months = Yellow
1 year = Moonglow

Men's Meetings

Usually closed, either discussion- or Step-oriented, these meetings are for men only so that they may feel more comfortable in their sharing and less distracted by the opposite sex. These are not to be confused with gay special interest meetings. They are most often attended by heterosexual men and are still sometimes, even in this day and age, known colloquially as "stag" meetings.

Women's Meetings

The same situation occurs for women as delineated previously for men. Customarily closed to nonalcoholics or nonaddicts, women's meetings render a "safe" atmosphere for women (again, normally straight women) to get together on their recovery, unhindered by distractions of the opposite sex.

> **Notes:** If available, single-sex meetings are a luxury we should not fail to utilize. Though it may sound sexist, most women early in recovery should routinely be steered in this direction. Women addicts and alcoholics do not have the same issues as men. There are different and sometimes more sexually specific hurdles they must face in coming to terms with their new recovering identity. Many have levels of shame and guilt that far surpass their male counterparts, given society's less than subtle and historically entrenched denigration of the "woman drunk" or the "prostitute addict." Being able to work this out within the safe company of other women is often critical.

H and I Meetings

"H and I" stands for Hospitals and Institutions. These meetings comprise a broad spectrum of groups that are essentially brought to another area, location, or facility. For example, "detox" meetings in hospital detoxification centers are H and I meetings, as are meetings brought to local jails and prisons by members of area Fellowships.

> **Notes:** By most accounts, anyone involved in "H and I" service work, as it is customarily referred to (it is also Twelfth Step work), is well on his or her way to recovery. People who do H and I service work are not to be confused with anyone, newcomer or not, who chooses to *attend* detox, institution, or facility-based AA or NA meetings. People who attend these meetings are certainly providing further evidence to others (i.e., in the hospital or institution) that the program works. They also get the benefit of seeing firsthand or remembering once again how bad it can get. However, those who are actually *bringing* these meetings to the group location, often leading the meetings or helping organize them, are the individuals who are doubly serious in their commitment to the Steps and the decision to "carry this message to alcoholics [or addicts]," a key part of the Twelfth Step.

Loner Meetings

Both AA and NA have components in place for people who are unable to physically get to meetings. For example, someone in the Fellowship who lives in a remote part of the world could express interest to headquarters and become a part of a loner group. They would receive names and addresses of other loners and nonloners choosing to participate. Recovering people are communicating with one another through the mail all over the world as part of this program.

Special Interest Meetings

There are meetings for doctors, lawyers, judges, pilots, gay men and lesbians, agnostics, atheists, foreign service officers, and people of other professions or philosophical orientations who feel compelled to join together in their recovery. Most of these meetings are not publicly advertised in a directory. One must find out about them by word of mouth.

PC-User Meetings

In this day and age of highly advanced information systems and the "information highway," it should be no surprise that most on-line public information services (e.g., CompuServe) have AA and other Twelve Step meetings available to PC users armed with a modem.

> **Final Notes on Meeting Types and Autonomy:** There are innumerable nuances to this concept of individual meeting autonomy. Some are more important than others and call for specific mention, as demonstrated above. Length of meetings also presents an interesting, but not particularly clinically significant, geographical variance. Some are an hour long; others are ninety minutes. There are smoking and nonsmoking meetings, the latter rapidly growing in popularity. Make no mistake about it, individual AA and NA groups do wind up creating their own reputation. Members talk about the relative merits of this meeting over that one. Some are considered "younger" than others, with fewer persons having long-term sobriety or clean time. Others are known for being chock full of old-timers, generally those in AA circles who have over twenty years' continuous sobriety.
>
> However, remember that there is no formal status based solely on length of sobriety. In fact, old-timers in AA often remind newcomers that they too are just one drink away from a drunk. Some say there is no such thing as a bad meeting, particularly if they stay clean and sober that day. Others will not be so forgiving about a particular meeting. But overall, and depending on geographic location and our knowledge as referral agents, there will be a meeting or group of meetings suitable for almost anyone.

Shaping the Referral: A Proactive Model

Refer; Re-Refer; and Re-Re-Refer

Those active in their Twelve Step programs often emphasize to one another, and particularly to newcomers, that "recovery is a process, not an event." This slogan is meant to reinforce the reality that there is no cure for the disease of addiction, that abstinence alone is not recovery, and that getting better over time takes exactly that: time. It is a process of growth, of change. It is not something that happens *to* people once they break out of denial and suddenly accept their addiction. Were it this simple, someone would have made a lot of money by now marketing the quick fix: one AA meeting, "I got it," and then you're outta there. Therefore, we need not fool ourselves into thinking that our initial referral will be *the event* necessary for adequate response by the offender. For most, it will be a *process* of referral, *re*-referral, and *re-re*-referral.

Resistance, denial, and prejudice will resurface in various forms, quite possibly continuing through to expiration of the case. Do not get discouraged. As stated earlier, there really is no such thing as an unsuccessful intervention. We may have planted a valuable seed, one that may not be harvested until long after supervision is terminated or even revoked. Our immediate challenge is to educate, and perhaps reeducate, all over again next week or next month, so that over time we lessen the impact of the offender's prejudice and initial resistance.

Referral Objectives

Obtaining a good drug and alcohol assessment to arrive at a treatment plan tailored to the individual client is standard practice in the addictions field. Client "A" may not have the same treatment needs as client "B." Social workers and other helping professionals emphasize the importance of starting where the client is *before* beginning therapy. Physicians diagnose or assess problems *before* they recommend treatment plans. Probation officers complete pre-sentence investigations *before* they commence supervision.

We must first practice assessment before defining our referral objectives for the individual offender. What's the purpose of my referral? Answering this question will likely determine the referral objective. By exploring it, we will make determinations as to the practical and procedural specifics of the evolving referral. Most important, we have to find out where the offender "is" at the moment of referral. For example, consider the following: We would not instruct a first-time nonalcoholic DUI offender to attend the recommended "ninety meetings in ninety days" of closed NA meetings. Not only is this the wrong program, but it is also overkill. Founded on faulty assessment, the result is a bad referral.

Our proactive model suggests that by determining the referral objective after assessment, we shape our decision about type of meeting(s), frequency of attendance, and overall level of involvement. Failure to tailor the outcome objective to the specific individual can be a certain setup for subsequent problems. Our personal and professional experience come into play over the life of the case as we move and shift in response to case circumstances and strike the proper balance between changing assessments and referral objectives.

"Standard" Referrals

Despite the fluid and changing nature of the referral process, there are some baseline considerations or standards that should assist us in arriving at a decision about whether or not to refer in the first place. Along with these standards are separate referral guideline questions, the answers to which shed light on how to proactively tailor a referral. Here are the standards:

STANDARD REFERRAL #1:

Refer anyone about whom there is the slightest suspicion of need, educational or otherwise. Remember: We have a professional obligation to ensure exposure to the program that works the best for most people, regardless of stage of disease, denial, or even treatment. When in doubt, refer to open AA/NA meetings! No harm can result.

STANDARD REFERRAL #2:

Refer anyone in active addiction or coming off a relapse. A recommendation for doing "ninety in ninety," or a meeting a day for at least three months, is often a good approach for an actively addicted offender—not as punishment but as an added recovery tool.

STANDARD REFERRAL #3:

Refer anyone upon discharge or termination from inpatient treatment, including hospitals, detoxification centers, and longer-term residential programs. At this point, these offenders have already been introduced to Twelve Step Fellowships and probably need only to be prodded.

STANDARD REFERRAL #4:

Refer anyone needing self-diagnostic assistance or individuals who question their drug or alcohol dependence, whether such assistance is voluntarily requested (it happens!) or is otherwise deemed necessary.

STANDARD REFERRAL #5:

Refer anyone who tests positive for an illegal drug or otherwise exhibits poor judgment vis-à-vis their drug of choice (e.g., visiting a PO under the influence of alcohol) while on community supervision. Using even once under the auspices of the criminal justice system signals a lack of control, prima facie evidence of dependence.

STANDARD REFERRAL #6:

Refer anyone out of prison or for whom it can be determined a problem existed at sentencing, regardless of length of time incarcerated. Addiction is a progressive disorder. It hangs around even when its victim is not using. Forced abstinence alone, even for very long periods of time, is not recovery.

Those are some general to-refer-or-not-to-refer standards. But what about the individual tailoring of a Twelve Step referral to meet a specific or court-determined supervision objective? What about the variety of referral options available in some areas? Should the offender be sent to AA, NA, or both? What about other programs from which the offender might benefit, such as those for sexual addictions, gambling problems, or compulsive spending? Should we insist on closed Step, open speaker, or beginner's meetings? How many meetings each week? Should sponsorship be encouraged? What about service work? How should attendance be verified, if at all?

We begin with the obvious: the *Who, What, Why* and *Where* words. Keep it that simple. People and conditions may be complicated; the questions to start with are not. And remember, it is a process. Start with where the offender is today. Tomorrow, or next month, the re-referral circumstances may look very different, just as our expectations might at the time. Here are the suggested questions, followed by several vignettes, to show how the answers help shape our referral "package."

WHO is the offender?

Consider age, sex, socioeconomic status, level of denial, Twelve Step literacy level, stage of recovery, cooperation level, motivation, and trustworthiness. These are but a few of the questions required to try and understand WHO the offender really is today and what he or she may need tomorrow.

WHAT is the drug of choice?

This is a basic question, but it is all too often neglected. Take the time to ask specific questions about alcohol *and other drugs.* Get comfortable with the offender's *current* drug-use pattern. If drugs other than alcohol are involved, look for a possible secondary relationship to alcohol.

WHY the referral?

Go back to the referral objective discussed previously. What is the purpose in making this referral? Is it to supplement an aftercare plan? Are you trying to help the offender self-diagnose? Is the objective abstinence-based or simply preventative or educational in nature? Is it court-ordered or probation officer-"suggested"?

WHERE can you refer?

What is available in the community? Perhaps one Twelve Step group is stronger than another, in terms of length of clean time of its members or cooperation with outside groups. Are there detox meetings, closed Step meetings, and clubs? Are there special interest meetings? Is it realistic to expect seven meetings a week when there are only three meetings in the area?

Now for some typical scenarios that highlight the importance of working these basic questions in actively shaping a Twelve Step referral package. Space allows for only a broad-brush examination. Keep in mind that there are as many different and unique referral constellations as there are addicted offenders. Try to individualize them. What is good for offender "X" may be contraindicated for offender "Y."

A Cocaine Addict

Consider the young adult businessman hooked on cocaine. He might do better in Cocaine Anonymous (CA) than Narcotics Anonymous. Since CA is available, we use it. Since AA is also well established, *and* the determination is made that the offender should abstain from alcohol (cross-addiction to alcohol is a reality in most cases), he is referred there as well.

Because the offender just completed an inpatient hospital stay, has two outpatient groups a week to attend, and has demonstrated trustworthiness in the past, we opt not to insist on having slips signed. Besides, we confer with outpatient staff and they assess whether or not he is in compliance. Incidentally, we know of no one who has ever truly embraced recovery, in the fullest sense of the word, without giving up all mind-altering substances, including alcohol in any form, regardless of the original drug of choice.

Of course our referral package demands a response to changing circumstances in the offender's recovery experience. For example, at some point we may become aware of secondary behavior problems, such as an emerging sexual addiction fueled by frivolous relationships within the Fellowship. We respond by encouraging the offender to discontinue or slow down the NA or CA involvement (the atmosphere of these groups, *in general,* is more sexually charged) in favor of more mainstream AA meetings.

On Methadone Maintenance

How about the heroin addict on methadone maintenance? Since there are Methadone Anonymous (MA) groups in the area, she might be better suited for MA than traditional NA. Moreover, we know this addict well, and we know that she will react negatively to the typical NA member's abhorrence of anything short of total abstinence, prescribed or not!

We still refer to AA as a supplemental recovery tool. Many ex-heroin addicts, some on methadone, some not, find themselves turning to addictive alcohol use. Those on methadone boost the effect with alcohol and catch a seductive high. Because the offender has not yet earned our trust and is very manipulative, we request submission of signed slips. We may also encourage the offender to have her MA sponsor check in with us, if willing.

Young Offenders

A young adult or teenager might do better at a young people's club, meeting, or group where there will be more emphasis on weekend activities such as drug-free dances and parties. Teenagers may also benefit from referral to companion Twelve Step family programs, like Alateen or Narateen.

Special Interest Groups

People whose professions or lifestyles make them feel too self-conscious in regular meetings may benefit from special interest meetings. Check your local desks or service centers for information on availability. Hesitate before routinely sending a lesbian or gay man to special-interest gay meetings. For some gay men and lesbians, this may be too distracting so early on because they may be tempted to form relationships with other members. On the other hand, straight men and women occasionally require same-sex meetings, for the same reason. Of course, fervent atheists will benefit from more secular-oriented Twelve Step groups available in many parts of the country.

Other "Referral Packages"

Someone who is already actively involved in a Twelve Step program, and has been for quite some time, will require little if any interference. We may wish to loosely monitor facets of his or her program like sponsorship and/or Step work. But enforcing signed slips for someone in this category would be unnecessary.

On the other hand, we often face the doubting, inexperienced, and frightened offender in need of a first-time referral. Consider starting off light, expecting attendance at a few open-speaker meetings. Suggest he or she pick up program literature to bring back as verification. Then, later, exercise the option of raising the ante and asking for slips, as well as encouraging attendance at closed meetings, perhaps several times per week. Someone in need of an educational experience, designed more for prevention than recovery, will benefit most from speaker meetings, open discussion groups, and perhaps less emphasis on slip-signing.

Actively addicted offenders in heavy denial may need a more hard-nosed approach: a direct referral to a specific meeting, closed or otherwise, where we know they will get the attention they deserve. Abstinence will be the bottom line, the ultimate goal. Firm instructions, accountability standards, and frequent attendance will be more characteristic of this scenario.

NA versus AA: Some Observations

Despite the implication, there is generally no competition or controversy between these two fellowships. However, there are noteworthy differences that complement one another. Before we discuss our observations, one thing should be made clear. As pointed out earlier, meetings and groups vary a great deal. Although it is dangerous to generalize, and we have consulted the NA World Service Office (WSO) for validation, these comments do not speak for either organization as a whole. They are based solely on the personal and professional experience of this writer.

Demographically, NA comes across to the casual observer as more "street-oriented." It is reasonable to assume that NA has more ex-offenders than AA.

Being a drug addict has certain realities, not the least of which has to do with being a part of the drug subculture. And for many in NA, the addiction to illegal or even prescribed drugs leads to the commission of a crime, whether it be for simple possession of a controlled substance or to generate income for drug purchases.

Some NA old-timers recall the days when their meetings were subject to surveillance by local police. After all, the prevailing opinion about drug addicts during the early days was very negative; the only thing worse than an alcoholic was a drug addict. During the 1950s there were "Rockefeller laws" that proscribed association with known criminals. Police would station themselves at predetermined meeting spots and harass participants or follow them after they left. NA's early history, were it formally recorded, would contain fascinating stories about their struggle to "come out" and be recognized as a legitimate recovery tool.

Uninterrupted chronological sobriety or clean time is generally less in length in NA than AA, at least within the United States. This is changing every year as NA matures and awareness about addiction and recovery increases. We would speculate NA's membership is younger than AA's, whose average age is forty-two, perhaps because illegal drugs such as crack cocaine (and others coming on the market) bring users to their knees much faster. Alcohol may take a full generation before deleterious effects or criminal behavior becomes apparent. Not so with many young drug addicts.

NA members appear to network and socialize outside the meetings more than AA members. There are frequent dances, special celebrations, and parties. AA does this too, especially some of the clubs populated by younger people, but as a whole there is not as much emphasis on *organized* outside social activity. Although AA is described as a "we" program ("I alone cannot recover, but we can"), NA seems to do a better job of outwardly emphasizing the importance of one's peer group or network. NA's decision to begin all but one of their Twelve Steps with *We* is another example. NA members also do more hugging. Whereas AAs hold hands at the close of a meeting, NAs often put their arms around each other in a circle. Men hugging men and women hugging women is not at all out of order, in either fellowship, really, but it does seem to occur more comfortably in NA.

Still there are *many more* similarities than differences. And it is not at all uncommon, depending on availability of meetings (AA tends to be more prevalent in most areas), for a person to attend *both* NA and AA. This may become more common as fewer "pure" alcoholics arrive on the scene. Usually, however, a person eventually focuses more exclusively on one or the other. (Incidentally, someone sincerely working the NA program will commit himself or herself to abstinence from *all* drugs, including alcohol.)

We should *never* persuade a person genuinely active in one fellowship or the other to make a switch. The operative phrase here is "genuinely active." Suggestions can and should be offered as to which fellowship might present a better match, depending upon one's individual issues or circumstances. What is important, particularly if offenders are beyond active resistance and attend meetings out of self-interest, is how comfortable they are where they are and whether or not they have "identified in."

Similarly, we should avoid discouraging drug addicts from attending AA meetings if they so desire. Leave the decision up to the offender. AA has not historically been overly receptive to polysubstance abusers. However, this is changing. There is much more tolerance for drug addicts in AA today than there ever used to be. Encourage the offender to identify himself or herself in the AA meeting as "an addict *and* alcoholic," or vice versa. Suggest that he or she not overdo it with the "drug-a-log." The key is that the offender is going to meetings. Period.

Program Options for Nonbelievers

There are instances when we encounter offenders who legitimately oppose and resist involvement in traditional Twelve Step groups. This opposition is based not on denial but genuine philosophical convictions about the recovery process. They may have honestly tried NA or AA but were unable to reconcile their own beliefs about religion and/or spirituality with the Twelve Step model. They are serious about abstinence, willing to look for outside help, and otherwise compliant with supervision standards—just not within the auspices of the Twelve Step approach.

One of the best resources for learning about recovery programs available to the nonbeliever is Rogers and McMillin's work entitled *Under Your Own Power.* They remind us that Twelve Step groups have historically been populated by many nonbelievers, including staunch atheists and agnostics. In fact, the *majority* of people coming to meetings for the first time fit into this category. So, despite the traditional Twelve Step group's resounding emphasis on spirituality, Rogers and McMillin write, "There are more atheists and agnostics within AA and its related organizations than in all other self-help groups combined."[1] Since there are legitimate alternatives to the traditional Twelve Step models, we would be remiss not to introduce them.

1. Ron L. Rogers and Chandler S. McMillin, *Under Your Own Power: A Secular Approach to Twelve Step Programs* (New York: Putnam Publishing Group, 1993), 51.

Rational Recovery (RR)

Rational Recovery (RR) appeared in the 1980s. It was founded by recovering alcoholics who rejected both the spiritual foundation of the AA Steps as well as the disease concept of alcoholism. RR patterns itself after the writings of Albert Ellis, a pioneer in the field of cognitive psychology and Rational-Emotive Therapy (RET). Like AA, RR groups vary widely, but they differ in some key respects.

Most RR members attend meetings only once a week, as opposed to the daily attendance schedule encouraged for newcomers to AA. RR has no equivalent to AA's large and open speakers meeting; in fact, the typical RR meeting more closely resembles an AA discussion group in size and tone. Meetings are generally limited to no more than twelve participants. Most AA members believe that alcoholism is a disease. RR members do not. They believe that problem drinkers make incorrect or shortsighted choices based on emotional states. RR is more time-limited while AA prefers to view itself as indefinite. RR members attend for six to ten months and then stop, sometimes returning to deal with specific crises or relapse. Finally, RR members do not see the necessity for a Higher Power; they emphasize an understanding of psychological issues that will return them to self-control.

Secular Sobriety Groups

Secular Sobriety was founded by James Christopher. He was in AA but left over his objection to the spiritual orientation of the Steps and the program's reliance on a Higher Power. Christopher believes that sobriety is best attained through an emphasis on self-reliance and self-knowledge. Secular Sobriety meetings resemble AA discussion groups. Most revolve around a sobriety-related topic, and there is substantial emphasis on practicing a daily program of recovery, including the focus on not taking a drink or drug no matter what the provocation.

Like AA, Secular Sobriety is based on the premise that alcoholism is a chronic and progressive disease. So unlike RR members, participants feel they cannot drink because of a physiological rather than psychological abnormality. One other distinct difference between Secular Sobriety and AA is Secular Sobriety's avoidance of traditional sponsorship.

Final Comments on Nonbelievers

In their book, Rogers and McMillin recommend that if nonbelievers choose to attend RR or Secular Sobriety, they should supplement their meetings with an appropriate Twelve Step group until sobriety is well established. The primary goal is to stay clean and sober, by whatever means. And there are certain advantages to being in the company of other recovering persons, regardless of one's philosophical objection to a Higher Power.

Finally, Rogers and McMillin point out three practical reasons for attending Twelve Step groups *even if a person doesn't believe in a Higher Power:*[2]

1. It's easier to find an AA meeting, and therefore sobriety. In fact, this is the most significant difference between AA, RR, and Secular Sobriety groups: AA's tremendous availability.
2. Twelve Step Fellowships are routinely very tolerant of different spiritual beliefs.
3. Twelve Step groups typically adapt to their members (e.g., polysubstance abusers, agnostics, and atheists).

Working *with* Resistance

Herein lies the raw essence of the referral process challenge: working *with* resistance. In many instances, denial manifests itself as pure resistance. The challenge is to work *with* it, move beyond it, and try something new, something foreign and, thereby, very threatening. In some cases, resistance will be the norm, regardless of the presence or absence of denial. An offender can be very honest about "owning" his or her addiction, even openly accepting the responsibility to take action, but still be resistant to acknowledging how Twelve Step groups might be of any help in the process.

Remember the subversive impact of the hidden message behind most of our Twelve Step referrals. Responding to such a suggestion or directive is not natural or comfortable. A person does not wake up with a Monday-morning hangover and proudly announce to friends and family that he or she has been inspired to try AA! It is an admission of abject defeat or capitulation, often shrouded in shame. We must respect the offenders' right to their resistance and do our best in the process to help them move beyond it. Here are some suggestions as to how we might work with typical offender responses to our inquiries about Twelve Step meeting attendance:

I went to a meeting BUT . . .

. . . I didn't like it; it didn't do anything for me.

Try responses such as, "You went to only *one* meeting?" (to confirm the fact that it was only one meeting); "Which one?" (to compare our knowledge of that

---

2. Rogers and McMillin, 81–82.

particular meeting, or type of meeting, with that of the offender); "What can't it do for you?" (to get a feel for what the offender's expectations are about program involvement).

Ask offenders to reserve their impressions of the program as a whole until they have taken in at least a dozen *different* meetings over the course of several weeks; or use Al-Anon's recommended "six weeks of meetings or six different meetings." Each meeting is autonomous; each has its own flavor, personality, and style. Encourage attendance at a variety of meeting types. Closed Step meetings tend to be smaller and promote more individual participation as opposed to the larger and usually open (nonaddicts welcome) speakers meetings. A combination of speakers, Step, and discussion meetings would be ideal. In some areas of the country you can find beginner's meetings, which focus on the first three Steps and can be very helpful to the newcomer.

. . . I couldn't stand the God-stuff. It's too religious for me.

Be prepared to persistently emphasize AA's *spiritual* foundation. It is *not* a religious program, and yet this is where many of us get stuck. Avoid religious debates with addicted offenders; AA and most Twelve Step programs demand nothing in the way of religious beliefs. Offenders are simply hearing people who *now* feel comfortable talking about their own personal concept of "God." Remind them of the phrase "Higher Power" introduced in the Second Step as something or someone other than "self." Or suggest they tune out the word *God* and make their Higher Power the meeting. AAs often say, "Take what you need, and leave the rest behind."

Make no mistake about it, *some* AA (and NA) meetings will leave the unwitting newcomer with the impression that having a belief in God and talking comfortably about God are part and parcel of being a "good member" of the Fellowship. Some groups do feel more spiritual than others, and, of course, depending on who volunteers to speak or share during these particular meetings, one might hear lots of God-talk. Remind the client that these are people who exercise their right to be more vocal about *their* faith, not AA's.

Again, we must do our homework and strive for an awareness of what types of meetings are available in our area. Know their reputations, some of their differences. Always remind the offender that it is dangerous to judge on a sample of one. Think about other options; maybe refer this offender to beginner's meetings, where the focus is usually on the first three Steps with much less emphasis on "God." If you have the sense this person is truly at odds with the entire spiritual undercurrent and will not move beyond it, consider trying to locate an agnostic meeting. If you look hard enough, and if you live in an area with lots of meetings, you may run across one.

. . . I couldn't relate to their "drunk-a-logs." Some of those people were really losers; I can see why they need help.

For your "higher-bottom" or lighter cases, caution them about "identifying out." Remind them of the progressive nature of addiction ("Once you've got it, you've got it") and that they should try to "identify in" by listening to feelings, emotions, or thinking patterns instead of circumstances. Suggest they listen carefully to how other members started drinking, what it was like in the beginning. They may find they have more in common with these "losers" than they thought. By choosing to recover now, they can avoid the "yet-to-comes." Finally, emphasize the educational aspect of attending meetings for those who are too arrogant or intellectual. Ask if there was anyone in the room they *might* have liked listening to, if they were really honest about it.

. . . I'm not drinking or drugging now, haven't for weeks. Besides, I go to those other classes [outpatient counseling] once a week.

As mentioned earlier, abstinence alone is generally not considered recovery. Do not be seduced into thinking that because an offender is not drinking or drugging that he or she is doing fine, is in recovery, and no longer needs to attend meetings. Despite our philosophical or etiological proclivities, most experts agree that addiction is multifaceted (emotional, biological, and spiritual). Recovery demands more than just ceasing ingestion of the mood-altering chemical. The Twelve Step program fills the gap and helps assure that a person stays sober, physically and emotionally. Since the Twelve Step group is not synonymous with professional treatment, avoid accepting an offender's assertions that he or she is substituting "group" or "counseling" for meeting attendance.

. . . I don't see why I need to go to meetings so often.

Be firm with your expectation that meetings be attended *frequently.* Most addicts manage to get high frequently, so there is nothing wrong with expecting or enforcing five to seven meetings a week or more. Most newcomers come every day of the week for their first year or two. The old AA adage "ninety meetings in ninety days" is a good starting point for the diagnosed chemically dependent. Perhaps require them to present slips for three or four meetings and get literature from the others (a way to get around the they-don't-sign-slips excuse).

. . . *I just can't get to them; I don't have the transportation or the money.*

How many times have we heard this? Here is a wonderfully practical Twelve Step program enigma: People in recovery *want and need* (recall the Twelfth Step) to "carry the message" to others. Calling upon fellow members to provide transportation will normally do more for the driver than the offender. It gives them the chance to give back what they have so freely been given. There is no inconvenience; this is something that must be repeatedly explained. Transportation is a nonissue, provided the newcomer expresses the desire to go to a meeting.

. . . *I can't handle saying, "My name is John, and I'm an alcoholic [or addict]." That's too much; I don't even know if I really am.*

There is no requirement that members must identify themselves like this. People often say, "My name is Bob, and I'm not sure . . ." Many of the people sitting next to the offender were in precisely the same place at some point in their sobriety. What the offender doesn't need to know is that exhibiting this type of honesty will likely result in *more, not less,* attention from others. AAs and other Twelve Step group members can be disarmingly sensitive and clever when it comes to greeting newcomers who prefer to think their attendance is but an embarrassing mistake.

. . . *I just sat there. No one paid any attention to me; they weren't very friendly or interested in me and that was just fine.*

It isn't "fine." We both know that, but sometimes it does take several visits before a person begins to feel like a part of the group. Take the time to encourage offenders to speak out in meetings. Tell them to ventilate their concerns about mandated attendance. Expressing doubts about being chemically dependent is also recommended. Just asking for help from the group to stay clean until they are off supervision is fine. Over time, the door will open for others in the meeting to approach and engage the newcomer in a way that may lead to friendship. Strongly suggest they attend the "meetings after the meetings," when group members gather at local restaurants for coffee and fellowship. The people who seem to make the best recovery in Twelve Step groups tend to formulate brandnew peer relationships.

. . . *There are really crazy people at that meeting; some that sure don't "walk the talk."*

Offenders commonly patronize people in recovery who "have" to go to meetings. Denial has many faces, as does resistance. "Selective" or "euphoric" recall is a phrase used to describe an early recovering addict's or alcoholic's propensity to remember only the good times associated with his or her drug or alcohol use. The pain, the guilt, the broken promises, and lack of control are facets of dependency that are stripped from memory. And so it goes with attending meetings early on. The same selective-recall mechanism ignites, in reverse, as the offender remembers only the negative aspects of these meetings.

Appeal for fairness, and suggest that this is why we insist they attend many different meetings and formats before they come to any final conclusion about the program as a whole. Acknowledge their observational skills. There *are* "crazy" people who go to meetings. After all, take any group of "normal" people, anywhere, and a certain minority of them are going to be different, more or less honest than their peers, and some certainly "crazier" than others. This is life.

Challenge offenders to discuss their opinions about groups of people in general, of their ability to sniff out superficiality, suggesting that in reality their discomfort may not have anything at all to do with people in recovery or people who attend *that* particular meeting. Help them get in touch with that part of their resistance masquerading as fear-inspired narrow-mindedness. Encourage them to use their heightened sensitivity to weed out the fraudulent, less sincere, or "crazy" people. Inspire them to find and stick with the winners.

. . . I prefer my outpatient group; after all, what good is it to sit around and listen to a bunch of dope fiends talking about their using—makes me want to get high.

This is a slight variation of the "crazy people" scenario previously described. As with many of these "resistances," first underscore the importance of reserving judgment until a representative sample of meetings has been taken in. Then discuss, perhaps all over again, the difference between a nonprofessional self-help group and outpatient treatment. Abstinence and outpatient counseling are the core components of this person's professional treatment, not AA or NA. They *are,* however, an integral part of the overall treatment plan: self-help groups to be utilized as tools for remaining abstinent and growing in recovery.

Discuss what happens after outpatient treatment has concluded. Talk about the importance of developing a new network of nonusing friends. Consider a suggestion that their euphoric recall, during the meeting itself, could be a dangerous indication of their emotional susceptibility to use again. In fact, this kind of statement is a dead giveaway for people in danger of relapse. They may not have "picked up" yet, but they are on the brink.

. . . I don't buy this stuff about powerlessness, not controlling things, and "turning it over." How can I turn my life over to anything and expect to get better? I'm the one who chooses to hit the pipe, and I'm the one who has to make the choice to stop.

This offender's attitude could be a lot worse. What comes across loud and clear, and is worthy of positive feedback, is that the offender *is* listening and paying attention. The statement suggests that he or she may have even glanced over program literature. However, and this is our challenge, how can we effectively reinterpret "powerlessness" and "turning it over" in a way that will have meaning to offenders as they exercise their "choice"?

Work with offenders to understand their resistance (and denial) through examination of drug-use patterns, control problems, and the negative consequences associated with continued use despite adverse consequences, all of which could be reframed within the context of powerlessness. Clarify, over and over again, that this does *not* mean the program strips its members of any control, personal choice, or decision making. It does mean that before they can start the recovery process, before they can get better, they must first "surrender to win." In so doing lies the motivation to try something different, *followed* by personal choice and willpower to carry it out. Following through with a commitment to attend frequent meetings takes *a lot* of willpower!

The paradox so difficult to grasp is that by learning to live by program principles, they are guaranteed the *power of choice* and the *power of freedom.* Suggest that "turning it over" to their Higher Power may mean any number of things. This is *their* decision. This is not an abdication of personal responsibility for recovery action. It is simply a courageous willingness to admit the truth: they cannot stop on their own.

Many addicts and alcoholics, comfortable in their recovery, talk about being "powerless over people, places, and things," as well as their drug(s) of choice. This is anathema to most newcomers still active in their addiction. Obsessed with control and power (over their drug of choice, primarily), newcomers find difficulty with the notion of giving this up, of accepting powerlessness and their true position in the world. Don't expect them to let go right away. At the very heart of this concept is the "Serenity Prayer," worth reprinting:

The Serenity Prayer
God, grant me the serenity
to accept the things I cannot change,
the courage to change the things I can,
and the wisdom to know the difference.

Help offenders reinterpret these words so they have *practical* meaning for them. For example, politely confront them on the fact that they are different from some others who consume alcohol or drugs. They get into trouble, unpredictably. They cannot change their body, their metabolism, or their family history of addiction. This is "straight up" the way it is: something over which they have no control. Neither can they personally change the criminal justice system, the trouble they are in now, or the "time" they must do under community supervision. But, if they are wise and bold enough, they *can* make the right decision about what they *can* change, what they *can* control this minute. They can choose to accept their addiction predicament for what it is—out of control—and ask for outside help to stay stopped. This *willful* decision yields the power that returns them to freedom.

. . . *I wanted to go to a meeting, but I was still drinking and drugging at the time.*

No problem. Remind this person of the Third Tradition: "The only requirement for membership is a *desire* [italics mine] to stop drinking [or using]." It does not say people must be abstinent before they are allowed to attend. Neither does it make a qualitative judgment about the intensity of the desire to stop drinking or drugging. It is ultimately an abstinence-based model of self-help if participants ever hope to avail themselves of its protracted benefits. However, as long as people are not disruptive to the meeting itself, they are welcome. So get offenders to the meeting, even if they are still drinking or using. They may hear exactly what they need to hear. Group members within a meeting have the capacity to skillfully (sometimes without ever directly confronting the person) address someone's active addiction in a way that opens the door for positive self-identification.

. . . *I was afraid I might see someone I know.*

This is a common fear. It isn't always expressed this way, but we should be aware of it. Ask what kind of meeting they attended. You'll find that most will reply "speakers," which are generally open to the public and therefore increase the newcomer's fear of being seen. Encourage the offender to find a closed meeting, particularly a Step discussion group. Anonymity will be at a premium here, and if someone does recognize the offender, remind him or her that others are there for the same reason he or she is. You should also remind the offender about Tradition Twelve and the value placed on the principle of anonymity. All groups, whether open or closed, are extremely sensitive to keeping what and who is seen, heard, or discussed within the meeting.

It is not unusual for this sensitivity and self-consciousness to be an issue in other places. Take, for example, the newcomer who attended a meeting the night before and is at the grocery store the next day with his wife and children. A person he met at the meeting approaches. In all likelihood, the acknowledgment of any association between the two will be left solely up to the newcomer; otherwise anonymity will call for only casual eye contact or a slight nod. Members of the Fellowship are surprisingly sensitive to the many shades of anonymity.

. . . *I felt cold stares when I started talking about my drugging.*

This *can* happen at an occasional AA meeting, if a person talks too much about the drugging side of his or her addiction. Some AA members, usually older ones, get concerned about their Fellowship being overrun by youngsters "into everything but alcohol." Encourage offenders to identify themselves as "an addict *and* alcoholic" if they are talking in a closed AA meeting. Suggest that they either make some reference to cross-addiction or perhaps keep their comments more to the feeling or "Step" level as opposed to offering a "drug-a-log."

. . . *I felt really uncomfortable being around so many men.*

Women offenders new to the process of recovery and Twelve Step groups in general, either AA or NA, often have just such a reaction. In most areas of the country, there *is* a preponderance of men in AA. It does seem to be changing. Slowly. Fortunately, and again this depends on where you are, there are a growing number of women's groups or meetings. Take advantage of them and refer.

In fact, for the average woman alcoholic or addict, attending a women's group should be a matter of routine. Women often have special needs that are better addressed within same-sex meetings. Society shames the woman alcoholic or addict more than her male counterpart. Be sensitive to this, not an unwitting partner to it. Women can also avoid the hassles of being "hit on," also known as "being Thirteenth-stepped," by going to same-sex meetings. They might feel more comfortable talking about and sharing histories of sexual or physical abuse within a more empathetic environment. Latest statistics reveal that at least two-thirds of women in recovery are victims of such abuse.

. . . *I can't find any good meetings in my area; they are so depressing. All they talk about is getting high and what it used to be like.*

First, find out exactly how many *different* groups or meetings this person attended. Often a comment like this is based on a single group experience.

Suggest he or she try out closed Step meetings or discussion groups. Some speakers meetings, as mentioned earlier, focus too much on using stories, what it was like *before.* Question the offender on his or her definition of a "good" meeting. Search for the real issue behind the resistance; something else is probably going on. Ask if there was a person who said something that struck a chord or hit home in some way. What was it that was said? Suggest he or she approach this person next time and ask about some "good" meetings in the area.

In many parts of the country, and certainly in larger metropolitan areas, there are "core" groups of recovering people who travel around together and find themselves consistently in the same meetings. Accordingly, an actively attending newcomer would observe several of the same faces throughout the week at different area meetings. So by asking a "regular" where else he or she goes throughout the week, the newcomer guides himself or herself toward the possibility of familiar faces and other "good" meetings.

. . . I really don't feel as though I fit in.

Again, suggest that the person think about approaching someone who said something he or she liked or didn't like at the meeting. It seems so obvious, but it isn't to the frightened newcomer. This is a practical technique to engage someone in conversation; most addicts and alcoholics are not great sober conversationalists. Any suggestions—the closer to actual "scripts" the better—will help the newcomer muster the courage to go up to someone he or she does not know and initiate conversation. Once a conversation is started, and once there is some give-and-take, the newcomer will probably feel better.

Not fitting in is to be expected this early on. Some meetings can be more cliquish than others. Listen, initiate conversation about the offender's concerns, and draw out specifics. Is it because the offender feels he or she is different, not alcoholic, not chemically dependent, or not quite as bad off? If this is the case, it might be time to start talking again about "identifying in" vs. "identifying out." Perhaps the newcomer is uncomfortable because group members are talking about the progression of their disease in a way that has not yet affected him or her. We can then re-emphasize the "not yet" portion of the equation and the fact that the addiction *will* progress if not treated. The newcomer can choose to get off the elevator now or wait until it plummets to the basement. Finally, note that perhaps the offender is uncomfortable because this is exactly where he or she should be at this time; it is hard to accept defeat and have to ask for help, no matter what the circumstance.

Slip-Signing Scams

The proverbial question remains: How do we tell if our offenders are *really* going to meetings? Slips or no slips, most of us suspect that a certain percentage of our drug-dependent offenders are providing us with fraudulent court slips. Or they mislead us with false information about their program involvement. We are right in our suspicions. It happens all the time and we do get fooled. But there are techniques we can practice to lessen the odds.

Before we move on, let us remember that AA and NA as a whole do not look disfavorably on the signing of court slips. Avoid over-identification with the offender, or the Fellowship as a whole, by concluding that due to the program's tradition of anonymity and nonaffiliation, mandatory referrals are somehow wrong or abusive. This is not so. AA and NA will take care of themselves. They have for many years, despite an onslaught of mandatory, community corrections-based referrals. *The Twelve Traditions are guidelines for AA and NA, not the criminal justice system.* We do not have the power to break their traditions; they do.

There will be certain meetings that send unwelcome messages to newcoming offenders who show up with court slips. Verify these occurrences and send them elsewhere. In most areas of the country, meeting availability will not present a problem, so this can be done without much trouble. Again, an individual group or meeting is perfectly within its rights (i.e., within the Twelve Traditions) to decide not to officially sanction the signing of court slips. AA and NA headquarters have no formal opinion on this matter; it is entirely up to the local group.

There are several ways around the "uncooperative" (our intention is *not* to sound pejorative) meeting or group, depending on the circumstances and individual offender. For one, coach the person into consistent attendance at the non-slip-signing meeting in question. Suggest he or she take a regular program member aside *after* the meeting and ask if he or she would be willing to sign the slip. Most individual members readily comply with such requests, particularly if they see the person showing up week after week. It's generally the *group* that does not want to condone wholesale slip-signing. Their concerns typically center around potential for disruption and an aura of cynicism that can envelop a meeting overpopulated by "slip-signers." Doing it discreetly, as suggested above, is another matter.

Another option would be to suggest the offender find an additional meeting, perhaps a smaller or closed meeting for the purposes of having the slip signed. As a general rule, it is the open meeting (probably speakers or discussion group) that may formally discourage court referrals. If the offender likes this particular meeting, encourage him or her to continue to attend without the slip. Have the offender keep his or her own record and be prepared to discuss the topic. Or direct the offender to bring program literature to the office as verification he or she was there. Another option is to suggest the offender find a sponsor from this meeting and have that person call and verify his or her involvement.

Always anticipate and be on the lookout for slip-signing scams. Most are fairly obvious to those of us who have been around a while. We see repetitive signatures, one meeting after another, listed as either "secretary" or "chairperson" of the meeting. The trouble is that the signatures look identical, each and every day. Same pen, same signature. Not likely.

Be careful with "club" or specific group "stamps"; they are often not very well supervised, and offenders can either make their own or secretly make repetitive stamps on their sheet. Keep in mind that a group with an official stamp is likely to be open. Look into it one day while in the neighborhood. Attend the meeting and see what the routine is.

Signatures with telephone numbers are a welcome sight, compared to the more nondescript and less personal stamp and date. Make the telephone call as verification. And again, this would *not* be a violation of a Tradition. It was that person's decision to put his or her phone number down; it is a statement of willingness to personally verify that the offender attended the group.

There are no set rules for signing, so varied forms of signatures should be expected. For example, question verification papers with *all* first names and last initials. AA and NA are anonymous, but not that anonymous in most big cities.

Pay attention to verification sheets that are too clean or not crumpled. Most offenders actually going to meetings and having their slips signed are putting that piece of paper to the ultimate test. See that it looks the part.

Look over the slips carefully. Pay attention to dates, names of meetings, and signatures. Look for discrepancies. Look for known meetings. Question offenders. Start a discussion concerning what they think of a particular meeting, whether or not they like this one or that one, how they feel about closed meetings versus open ones. Rely on professional intuition to help determine the veracity of their responses.

Use area meeting directories to cross-check the ones listed on an offender's verification sheet. Do it while the offender is still present so that he or she sees you mean business and are serious about the referral. Avoid communicating distrust; rather, say something to the effect of, "Oh, I wasn't aware of that meeting. Is that one in the directory? Where is it? I'm curious."

What is the best way to tell if someone is really attending Twelve Step meetings? One word says it all: *change.*

For some it will be more dramatic than for others. At minimum, there will be a sense of open-mindedness and willingness to become a different person. At best, there will be *comfortable* abstinence and a decision to work the Steps as means of maintaining it. For those brave offenders who are indeed trying to change lifestyles, cognitive patterns, and remain abstinent all at the same time by going to meetings and getting involved in their Twelve Step program, the question as to *verification* of attendance will not even come up. Their decision to embrace the Fellowship will be obvious.

What about the others, the ones who are going only because they are forced to attend? What about the ones who have one foot in and one foot out of the meeting rooms? Or those who consistently forget their slips, but who we suspect are in fact going? Here are four key questions, under the acronym SOAR, which we may use as a framework to guide our assessment effort to determine someone's involvement in AA *without using court slips.*

The "SOAR" Questionnaire
(A Quick Assessment and Discussion Guide for Determining Twelve Step Program Involvement)

1. Do you have a **S**ponsor and work the **S**teps?

2. How **O**ften do you attend meetings?

3. How **A**ctive are you in the Fellowship?

4. How do you **R**elate to others in the meetings?

Each of these questions represents a level of involvement in the Twelve Step program.

Commitment Level

1. Do you have a **S**ponsor and work the **S**teps?

Determine the newcomers' commitment level by focusing on the following questions: Ask if they have found a sponsor. If not, why not? Do they plan on finding one at some point in the future? What's holding them up? Ask what they think about sponsorship in general, why people find it a help.

Ask about participation in Step meetings. Do they know what a Step meeting is about? Ask. Do they attend Step meetings or go only to open speakers meetings? Are they working any of the Steps now? What Step might they see themselves working on these days? What are the first three Steps? What does it mean to "work the Steps," anyway?

Note that most offenders who find sponsors, get involved with a sponsorship network, and work the Steps are very committed to their program.

Frequency of Attendance

2. How **O**ften do you attend meetings?

Get specific about it. Generate a conversation on the topic and don't let up until you're satisfied. Ask newcomers what kinds of meetings they attend. If they cannot list some of the different types (open, closed, discussion, Step-study, and so on), we have reason to question. If they pause and think, "Well, I go to one or two a week usually," they are likely minimizing their attendance and almost certainly are not involved.

Ask whether or not they have a "home group." If they look at us quizzically and cannot respond, we learn something. Ask how many meetings other people in the program attend. Ask why they think people still go to meetings years after they are "sober." Ask them why they shouldn't be attending "ninety meetings in ninety days," particularly if they were using every day. Someone who is attending a lot of meetings (five to twelve a week), especially early on, is committed to the recovery process.

Participation Level

3. How **A**ctive are you in the Fellowship?

Focus on questions designed to determine whether or not the offenders have become involved in "service work," like making coffee, becoming a program chair (finding persons to lead meetings), volunteering to be a secretary for a meeting (collecting donations for expenses, keeping the books, and so on), or serving as a General Service Office (GSO) representative.

Consider asking questions about whether or not they have led meetings, told their story, or "Twelfth-Stepped" anybody new to the program. Do they go to "meetings after the meetings" or to group-sanctioned social outings like dances, spiritual retreats, or conventions? Answering yes to any one of these questions suggests active participation and genuine commitment.

Identification Level

*4. How do you **R**elate to others in the meetings?*

Try to get a feel for their level of identification as a recovering or recovered addict or alcoholic. Do they identify with the recovery process? With specific people in the meetings? Are they "identifying in" by making connections to their own circumstances, powerlessness over drugs, or emotional pain? Or do they see themselves as outsiders looking in on a process that is "okay for those who need it, but not for me." This is sometimes referred to as "comparing out."

Offenders willing to admit and talk about their identification with other recovering addicts and alcoholics are well on their way toward breaking through denial, gaining acceptance of their addiction, and moving into the recovery phase. Answering the SOAR questions to our satisfaction will not be proof positive that an offender is attending meetings. But used as a framework for generating a discussion, SOAR will have practical utility. If nothing else, try using it as a guide to assess an offender's level of denial and attitude about addiction.

Sponsorship: Use It or Lose It!

> *So, this is the fourth time you've picked up a thirty-day chip. Now I'm not telling you anything, but I would like to make a simple suggestion. Just a suggestion, all right? If I were you, I would get real busy sponsoring somebody! I know you have a sponsor. That's not the problem. He's staying sober, because he's sponsoring you. You're not. Again, I'm not telling you to do anything. I am strongly suggesting that if you really want what we have, you start by sponsoring someone right away. Why now, this early in the game? Because I guarantee you, absolutely guarantee you, that if you do, you won't get drunk. He might, the person you sponsor. But that's okay. You won't. I don't care if all you have is twenty-four hours and the guy you sponsor has six hours! That's the essence of this deal: get out of yourself and*

help another drunk. Again, I'm not telling you to do anything, right?
> *—An "old-timer" to a newcomer in an AA meeting*

Of course the old-timer is doing just that: telling the newcomer he must get serious about his program or else. Although becoming a sponsor is often better deferred to a time when a measure of sobriety and experience with the program have been achieved, the old-timer's point is still valid: The newcomer had better start thinking about applying the Steps to his life by offering to help someone else, by thinking beyond his own circumstances, and by reaching out to another suffering addict. What the old-timer is suggesting is that the newcomer get up off his duff and into action.

Such "eldering" (not an AA term but quite appropriate, it seems) stretches the boundaries that normally discourage "cross-talk" or back-and-forth conversation between group members during a meeting. Confrontation and direct person-to-person "counseling" form the basis for traditional group therapy, but not for AA and most other Twelve Step groups. The message comes across more subtly, but perhaps even more powerfully, through someone else's testimony, through their sharing.

The Point and the Paradox

Sponsorship is *always* successful as long as the sponsor stays clean and sober. The reason the sponsor stays clean and sober is by virtue of the *act of* sponsorship. By "giving up what was once so freely given," they say, one is able to keep it. It is a simple enough concept but thoroughly beyond the grasp of most newcomers. The sober-*less* thought goes like this:

> *I can't possibly call this guy when I want to drink or drug. He's busy. He works. I get cravings late at night. Who am I kidding? I can't bother him. I still have some pride left.*

Yes, probably sufficient pride to kill oneself. But if the recovering person finds the courage to call, this is what may happen. The newcomer goes on and on for thirty minutes talking about his or her day, the compulsions, the worries, the resentments. The sponsor says very little, if anything. The newcomer begins to feel better, the urge to use diminishing with each word. But then pride resurfaces as he or she recognizes that this stranger on the other end of the phone just gave up thirty minutes of his or her time to hear this "babbling." The newcomer says to the sponsor, with all sincerity, "Thanks so much for listening." Curiously, the sponsor comes right back and replies, "No, no, thank you for keeping me sober today." The newcomer hangs up the phone and feels better, a little more confused, but willing to try it again sometime. It worked, and he or she earns another day of sobriety.

What Is Sponsorship and Why Get into It?

Historically, sponsorship is where it all began. It was Bill Wilson who "sponsored" Dr. Bob Smith during the early days of AA. Bill was in the midst of a serious craving for alcohol when he thought, "You need another alcoholic to talk to. You need another alcoholic just as much as he needs you."[3] Both men actively sponsored hundreds of others to sobriety as the Fellowship gained ground. This was the *key* to their sustained sobriety: one addict or alcoholic talking to another, passing on his (it was *"his,"* in the early days) "experience, strength, and hope." Sponsorship is often but not always the *primary vehicle* for passing recovery on, for relaying the message to someone new and keeping recovery alive for *both* persons. This is why sponsorship is so important.

Unlike in many other organizations, sponsor and sponsee in AA meet as equals. There is no authority line. One does **not** *have to have* a sponsor to be a member of AA or any other Twelve Step group. However, it does come highly recommended. A 1992 survey conducted by AA indicated that 78 percent of members had a sponsor and that 72 percent of those got their sponsor within ninety days.

Who Is a Sponsor?

A sponsor is someone who has "been there," someone with whom the offender can relate. *We have not been there.* We have not experienced it. And for some of us it is very difficult to comprehend why anyone would continue to do something that could jeopardize his or her freedom in the community. Sponsorship moves beyond that and places the offender right where he or she should be: in the midst of a relationship with a peer, with another drug addict or alcoholic who is "doing the right thing" and working the program.

A sponsor is someone who has been around "the rooms" a while, working the program. Most experienced sponsors have demonstrated their understanding of the Steps and have put them to practice in their own lives. It is recommended that a sponsor be someone who has a few years of sobriety or clean time, a person willing to offer an insider's view, perhaps become a friend or mentor to the incoming

---

3. As written in the AA General Service Conference-Approved pamphlet entitled *Questions and Answers on Sponsorship*, from which a significant portion of this section on sponsorship has been adapted.

offender. Again, there are no formal rules. In fact, a sponsor could have *less* clean or sober time than the person he or she is sponsoring. This might be the case a few years into recovery, when the person with fifteen years' sobriety decides to ask a friend at the meeting who has only nine years' to sponsor him or her. It happens. Certainly the quality of clean and sober time is more important than the actual number of years.

A newcoming offender is just that—new. There is a lot to learn about the Twelve Steps, the various meetings in the area, and the subtle nuances of a particular group. A good sponsor will offer time (and availability), friendship, and acceptance. He or she will walk newcomers through the Steps, perhaps have lengthy conversations with them about how he or she worked through his or her own denial and resistance to going to meetings.

Most sponsors offer lots of suggestions. Some will be very direct and instructive in their approach. Others will be less authoritative. Some newcomers find they benefit more from a hard-nosed or parent/child style of sponsorship. Others gravitate toward the non-directive relationship with a sponsor who offers not so much answers as options.

A sponsor is not a choice made for life; it is not a "forever" friendship. Many newcoming offenders get confused about this and complicate or prolong the decision making process. Sponsors change, sometimes often, throughout the course of one's recovery. People five years into the program may no longer struggle with the basics. Perhaps they arrive at a point where they come face-to-face with a stubborn spiritual emptiness. "Clean for five years and all I get is this. . . . I still feel empty. . . . What am I doing wrong?" The decision to search for a new sponsor, or even an additional one (there are no rules prohibiting multiple sponsors), would be very wise in this situation. Finally, *every "good" sponsor should have* his or her *own sponsor.* Sponsoring others without having one's own sponsor is considered dangerous territory.

Newcomer Offenders: Q's & A's on Sponsorship

Here are common questions and concerns about sponsorship raised by offenders who are new to Twelve Step programs. Note the resistance and fear. Imagine being twenty-eight years old, "grown-up," and having to ask someone to sponsor you. It is not an easy task. So in response to some questions we should look beyond the surface and sensitize ourselves to the underlying concerns.

How do I find a sponsor? (Or, "I don't trust anyone.")

There are as many ways to find a sponsor as there are meetings in an area. The quickest way is to attend meetings frequently. Emphasize listening to others in the meeting and sharing. Stress going to closed meetings, where the offender is likely to find more people serious about recovery. Some very large (and open) speakers meetings have sponsorship lists and focus on this aspect of the program. Recall the old adage "You can't con a con." Remind offenders that before long they will know who is really "walking the talk." Suggest they start collecting phone numbers and calling. All of this prep work will help them quickly come to a decision about sponsorship.

I'm looking for a sponsor but haven't found one yet.
(Or, "I'm afraid of being rejected.")

Offenders will procrastinate. Expect it, but do not encourage it. Insist that they find one soon. Many newcoming offenders act as if they are "terminally unique" or somehow special. They hide behind this notion and use it as a rationalization to put off finding a sponsor. They say they cannot find someone good enough to *address their particular problem.* Or they project a fear of rejection. For some, asking another person to sponsor them is like asking for a date. We must be aware of this and not minimize the potential emotionally charged subtleties. Suggest "temporary" sponsorship, and remind the offender that this is not a forever friendship. Recognize and legitimize their concern about rejection, but do not buy into their resistance.

Do not underestimate the anxiety involved in this proposition. Directly ask offenders how they plan to approach their potential sponsor. Perhaps we can help by making suggestions as to how they phrase the question. Openly confront and talk about possible rejection. Is it really a *personal* rejection? What if the person is holding down two jobs and already sponsoring a number of people? Talking about the process, breaking it down for them, and anticipating possible scenarios can help.

Is it okay for me to have more than one sponsor?
(Or, "Don't get too close to me.")

NA and AA vary on this one. NA suggests only one sponsor, because it is easier to trust one person than many. Also, by having more than one sponsor a person may be tempted to selectively disclose parts of himself or herself to various sponsors, which could be limiting and ultimately self-defeating.

On the other hand, AA feels that a newcomer who has more than one sponsor avoids the situation of being caught in a bind and not having someone available during a craving or difficult time. The newcomer will also share in a wider variety of individual AA experiences by having more than one sponsor.

Keep these considerations in mind when talking with offenders new to sponsorship. Then make suggestions based on the individual needs of offenders and/or their personalities. For example, a newcomer may unconsciously hide and avoid formation of a purposeful sponsorship relationship with any *one* individual, favoring superficial relationships with several. In such a case, you may want to recommend a single sponsor with some backup names to contact in a crisis situation.

Is it okay to have a friend sponsor me?
(Or, "I much prefer a friend; he or she won't push me where I don't want to go.")

No, this is not recommended. Trust is vital, but asking a friend or family member to be a sponsor is not a good idea. This implies prior association, perhaps a previous history of using together, a codependent relationship, and certainly the possibility of other relationship issues. The trouble is that these issues will resurface in strange and usually disruptive ways.

Newcomers are more likely to follow the *objective* guidance of a trusted but unknown sponsor than advice from someone whose background or prior relationship with them may have already been compromised. Building *new* interpersonal trust is so important to the process and becomes dangerously moot if the choice for sponsorship comes down to a friend or relative.

Should my sponsor be a man or a woman?
(Or, "Please say it's okay for me to ask the opposite sex; I can handle that!")

There is no disagreement on this one: early on, sponsorship should *always* involve members of the same sex. This puts to rest certain sexual distractions and prevents unnecessary emotional confusion. The goal is to develop a meaningful same-sex bond, an honest relationship unencumbered by power politics or sexual conflict. Both risk in the sharing process, and both learn about nonsexual, nonphysical intimacy and friendship. This is unfamiliar ground to many addicts and alcoholics prior to recovery.

There are people who have been clean and sober for several years who opt for sponsorship by the opposite sex. However, their decision is typically based upon distinctive or recovery-specific reasons, such as the sponsor's expertise or style in a particular facet of their recovery.

Professional Parameters on Sponsorship

Sponsorship cuts to the very core of the recovery process: two people with the same problem talking to one another about how to save their lives and live life *comfortably*. As criminal justice professionals, no matter how skilled, we will never have such one-to-one impact. Fortunately, for most of us anyway, our credentials don't include the same devastating historical experience with addiction.

What we *can* do is assume a proactive role in guiding and encouraging newcomers to take advantage of this facet of their program involvement. Recovery without sponsorship is a setup for failure. To the extent that we can foster this attitude among our addicted offenders, the more likely their chances for sustained abstinence. Here is a list of practical supervision techniques that help define our professional parameters on the sponsorship issue.

- *Simply going to meetings is not enough in most cases.* Be careful not to compromise in this area. Push the offender to get a sponsor. Right away. Ask about it again and again. Talk about it each visit until satisfied that the offender has correct information.

- *Stress that sponsorship helps the sponsor, that "inconvenience" is a nonissue.* Sponsors, by giving back what they have received from their sponsors and the Fellowship as a whole, are able to stay clean and sober *by helping someone else*. Most, if not all, newcomers to Twelve Step programs have this paradoxical abhorrence of "using" others in recovery. It's fine to use others and take advantage of people during an active addiction, but many do not dare summon the strength to ask for help in recovery! Talk it out. Discuss the paradox and stress the underlying courage required of them to fulfill this part of their program.

- *Encourage the offender to have his or her sponsor call the office.* This is not appropriate to mandate, for an offender's sponsor is not the one on supervision. It *is* an anonymous program and a sponsor is entitled to his or her anonymity. But there is nothing wrong or contrary to the Traditions with encouraging an offender to solicit his or her sponsor's cooperation in this regard. Most are more than willing to cooperate. Be sensitive and keep the questions simple and not clinically oriented. We are interested in compliance, abstinence, and meeting attendance, not secrets or intimacies.

- *Be creative and proactive.* Establish special programs to help widen the pool of available sponsors. For example, the U.S. Probation Office for the District of Montana recently established a "Binding the Gap" program. By working closely with the local H and I committee of AA, and after appropriate background investigations, the office compiled a list of volunteer sponsors. They in turn make a commitment to sponsor an inmate close to release. Probation officers then match up individuals prior to their release on community supervision. This way offenders already have a temporary sponsor at the time of their first report to the office, someone who is ready to assist with the transition back to the community.

- *Make use of other offenders on supervision who have demonstrated an honest commitment to the program.* This calls for obvious professional discretion (and appropriate screening), but we do often fail to take advantage of what could be our closest allies (or human resources!)—those offenders who have made it and are ready to start sponsoring others. Provided criminal-association rules are relaxed, and as long as it is thoroughly discussed with management (or the court, or paroling authority, as the case may be), consider arranging an introduction between a newcomer and an offender involved in a Twelve Step program. After clearing it with the potential temporary sponsor, have them exchange telephone numbers and call each other. Suggest they go to a meeting together.

- *Be patient and persevering with offenders on the subject of sponsorship.* Make it real for them. Explain and explain again their obligation to *aggressively* seek sponsorship. Communication is paramount, both as it relates to the sponsorship process as well as our working relationship with the offender. Who takes the first step in finding a sponsor? It is not uncommon for newcomers to think that they must be approached, that they must wait. Or, as mentioned earlier, they may have grandiose notions about who might be appropriate for them. So we counsel them to initiate the phone call or conversation, to approach the potential "temporary" sponsor. They are to ask the questions. They are to reach out and ask for help. The Fellowships are not churches; they do not proselytize, and waiting too long could be costly.

- *Remember that a sponsor is not a professional caseworker, therapist, or counselor.* A sponsor is not someone from whom the offender is supposed to borrow money, clothes, or food. Neither are sponsors there to provide legal, domestic, religious, or medical advice. Certainly, sponsors provide a safe place to discuss a variety of sensitive topics. They are meant to be a guide to recovery through the Twelve Steps.

Wrapping It Up with "Do's and Don'ts"

Finally, and as means of summarizing the most important aspects of our proactive referral model, we provide the following list of "do's and don'ts":

- ***Don't*** *rush the referral process.* Find the time to talk to offenders about the Twelve Step programs. Listen to their objections. Talk about their stereotypes and misconceptions. Accept the challenge to educate them, and *be enthusiastic* about it! It might be contagious. Furthermore, ask questions and solicit information from those who have turned the corner and made participation in the Fellowship a way of life. Listen and learn from them, too. See if they will share their story with you.

- ***Do*** *prepare and plan.* Have area directories on hand with specific meetings highlighted in an offender's neighborhood. Explain the various meeting types. Keep a record of "good" meetings, ones that others have talked about, and pass it on to the newcomer. Have Twelve Step literature on hand such as the Big Book (AA), the Blue Book (NA), and various pamphlets. Advise your indigent offenders that many of these may be picked up at no cost once they express interest and attend a meeting.

- ***Don't*** *view Twelve Step meetings as "punishment."* Avoid this as much as possible. Coming from this perspective, an impartial and professionally appropriate referral is not likely. If we think of AA as punishment, we will be unable to inspire enthusiasm, objectivity, or cooperation. There will be ample resistance as it is; there is no need to fire it up.

- ***Do*** *tell addicted offenders there are no minimum requirements for meeting attendance.* In fact, there are only two times offenders *must* go to meetings: first, when they want to, and second (and especially), when they don't want to! The more the better. One rule of thumb is to consider how often a person used during his or her active addiction. For example, if an offender got high or used on a daily basis, then it is reasonable to expect daily meeting attendance.

- ***Don't*** *make the mistake of not wanting to "intrude" on an "anonymous" program.* This is a major error promulgated by far too many criminal justice professionals, especially probation officers. There is an unfounded hypersensitivity to the anonymous nature of the Twelve Step program that ends up inhibiting our willingness to encourage or mandate attendance. Remember, the Twelve Traditions and the principle of anonymity governing the Twelve Step meetings are for *their* protection, not ours. We have every right to use them for addicted offenders, either as a primary recovery mechanism or as a viable secondary support system to complement professional treatment.

> *Note:* To those who have legal concerns about whether or not mandatory self-help group attendance violates the Establishment Clause of the First Amendment to the U.S. Constitution, please review details under "Note" in chapter 3, page 58. In 1994 a federal judge ruled in favor of mandatory self-help group meetings.

- *Do routinely ask about length of sobriety.* Offenders who know their anniversary date or even count the individual days tell us something about their commitment to abstinence. Congratulate them. Reinforce and encourage them. Length of sobriety (though certainly not always the truth, of course) helps us gauge an offender's progress.

- *Do think about creative ways of interacting with area Twelve Step programs.* For example, consider bringing meetings to the office or institution, having follow-up Twelve Step meetings after professional outpatient group counseling (take advantage of a captive audience!), developing sponsorship or "binding the gap" programs, or inviting panels of recovering persons from the community to come and talk to staff about their respective Twelve Step groups.

- *Don't underrefer.* Making the referral and introducing the addicted offender to the Twelve Step groups available within his or her community should be our *primary obligation.* It will not be for everyone, we know. But initially the choice should not be up to us. The addicted offender will help us make this decision later on. When the offender is first seen by correctional staff (e.g., intake), referral to the appropriate program should be standard procedure.

- *Don't easily rule out AA and NA.* Most of us know or have at least heard about Rational Recovery (RR), and other secular groups. Whenever we make such referrals, consider supplementing them with AA or NA meetings. RR meets only once a week in most areas; what about the other six days?

- **Do** *stress that first-time referrals do the following:*
  - Attend ninety meetings in ninety days ("90 in 90") initially
  - Arrive early and stay late
  - Attend a combination of meeting types (open, speakers, Step, Big Book, and so on), at least initially
  - Find a "home group" ASAP (see glossary for definition)
  - Get a sponsor
  - Get program literature
  - Work the Steps
  - Get involved with "service work" (making coffee, acting as program chairperson, and so on)

- **Don't** *ever allow newcomers to render an opinion on the basis of a couple of meetings.* All too often we buy into the offenders' premature belief that the meetings are "just not for me." We discover their judgment is based on having gone to a "couple" of meetings. Insist that newcomer offenders take in *many* different meetings at first. Suggest that they shop around and reserve their opinion for later. In many parts of the country there are as many different meetings as there are prospective newcomers on our caseload. Chances are, we can help them find the right match.

- **Don't** *settle for "controlled drinking" or "light drug" use as representative of true program commitment.* Both AA *and* NA are *no* drinking and *no* using programs. Do not discourage people from attending simply because they are still using, but be cognizant of the fact that Twelve Step meetings *are* abstinence-based. Not only does scientific research support the potential for cross-addiction, but the sheer wealth of personal experience shared by legions of recovering people have told the same story, over and over again: *secondary drug use inevitably leads a person back to his or her drug of choice.* Consider the example of the cocaine addict, abstinent from her drug of choice for several months, who makes the ill-fated decision to start "chipping" on marijuana or alcohol. She controls it *temporarily;* after all, she never really had a problem with alcohol or dope, anyway. We know the rest of the story.

- **Do** *point out the "powerlessness paradox."* Many first-time referrals react negatively to the frequent use of the term *powerlessness*. They see it written in the First Step. They hear about it frequently in First Step meetings and beginner's meetings. They hear it in the phrase "powerlessness over people, places, and things." Most of us are taught early on to be self-sufficient, to use willpower to confront a personal problem or goal. In our culture, powerlessness is anathema. Many of us avoid discussion of this potential stumbling block to someone's Twelve Step participation. Instead, point out that the word *powerlessness* simply cuts to the core of their addiction, no more, no less. Then hypothetically challenge them to prove differently in terms of their drug-use pattern. Suggest looking at it in terms of a "sporadic control problem" at first, if powerlessness has such negative connotations. Or make the chocolate analogy: *If every time you were to eat a chocolate bar you became very sick, how difficult would it be for you to remain forever abstinent from chocolate?* Do they see the difference?

Remind them that this term has nothing to do with the tremendous strength and willpower these offenders have in *other* areas of their lives; they are powerless over their active addiction (i.e., they have serious *control* problems), not their lives today, whether or not they will attend meetings, or how they choose to respond to their treatment program requirements. By having enough raw courage to admit defeat, to admit powerlessness over drugs or alcohol once in their system, they ultimately gain the greatest power of all: *freedom*.

- **Do** *allow certain offenders the freedom to attend meetings on their own.* Do not be too rigid about slip-signing. Practice authenticating meeting attendance by interview techniques, with or without slips. Professional discretion will dictate those circumstances when an offender may be ready for such latitude. But right now they may need to demonstrate that they are going to meetings *for* themselves and not the system.

- **Do** *talk about why many recovering addicts still go to meetings.* Point out why so many addicts, long after they experienced their last compulsion to drink or use drugs, continue active involvement in the Fellowship. Touch on the importance of "passing it on" as insurance for keeping it. Point out that for most of the people in this category, the *easiest* thing they do every day is *not* take a drink or drug; the challenging part for them, and why the program becomes such an integral part of their lives for years and years, is how to live life comfortably, how to interpret the Twelve Steps into a meaningful and purposeful sober life.

Chapter 6

Companion Community Resources

Introduction

The effects of alcoholism and drug addiction are rampant within the offender population. This we all know. The supporting facts and statistics are conclusive no matter where you turn. As criminal justice professionals working within the correctional community, we accept it. In fact, for some of us who have been around a while, it takes on an aura of intuitive reality. We must only rarely be reminded that the main focal point of our work, both in the community and the office, nearly always hovers around the *individual* addicted offender.

However, we focus so much on the individual offender and his or her addiction that we miss one of the most important components of addiction and recovery: the family, as defined in its broadest context, including spouse, significant other, sibling, child, or other loved one. Typically, we have neither the professional resources nor the time to reach out to what some may argue are these more legitimate victims of substance abuse in the first place. Yet reach out we must; because not only does the family hold a pivotal position relative to an offender's recovery, *but it also stands to perpetuate the cycle all over again.*

So the challenge we face here is how to balance the often conflicting family dynamics that threaten to offset potential gains made by an addicted offender. Even though the addict's family may have been seriously victimized by the disease of addiction, they often work unwittingly *against* recovery. The reality is that no matter how hard we might work with an individual offender, if the family members are largely unsupportive and/or not recovering, chances are that even our best individual counseling skills or supervision techniques will not overcome their negative influence. Remember that addictive disease neither initiates nor perpetuates itself within a vacuum—families are unconsciously adversarial as well as consciously supportive—and *the family of the addicted offender is as much in the dark about the nature of addiction and recovery as is the offender himself or herself.* If some effort is not made toward helping family members and significant others get to the point where they are "reading off the same page," relapse is nearly inevitable.

Fortunately, we have options to pursue. Companion community resources, such as AA's partner fellowship, Al-Anon; NA's partner fellowship, Nar-Anon; and other family-oriented Twelve Step self-help groups, are there for us as tremendous resources for both the family and friends of the addicted offender. It is no secret that Al-Anon and Nar-Anon are both seriously underutilized. If we hope to maximize our effectiveness with individual offenders, we must provide fertile ground within which they can recover *as a family.*

We know that experts who oversee residential treatment programs try hard to re-create a family-like milieu and supportive atmosphere for the recovery process. Patients are encouraged to build trust, practice self-disclosure, and share pain. This is done for an important reason. The family, real or therapeutically contrived, is a powerful motivator. Human beings are indisputably social animals; we thrive on the love, support, and fellowship of our brothers and sisters (literally and figuratively). We feel good about ourselves when supported by other people. For most of us, the prospect of living in isolation, away from family or friends, would be tantamount to death. Who would we impress? Who would we nurture? Who would make us sad? Who would motivate us? Who would make us feel warm and needed? Who would we respect? Who would respect us?

Drug- and alcohol-addicted offenders are no different and typically find "family" in the context of their using friends or street relationships, as well as enabling family members. In the professional jargon we talk about "negative peer relationships." We see offenders complete rehab or incarceration, vow to stay away from "negative people," and then promptly find themselves right back in the saddle. Their street family is comfortable, good or bad. Couple that powerful inclination to return to what is comfortable with what we know about addiction as a disease, and you have a prescription for relapse again and again.

The Addicted Family System

How does chemical dependence or addiction affect the nonaddicted spouse, sibling, or loved one? Here are some real-life vignettes reprinted from the pages of

Al-Anon and Nar-Anon literature to help personalize and give the family members' struggles meaning:

An Al-Anon member:

> *When I started with the group I was ill—physically and mentally. My life was one mad obsession—my husband's alcoholism. The neglect of my children and myself was a frightening thing. Fear is contagious and our home was full of fear. I was aware of it, but could do nothing. The shame, the fear of the future—I need not explain.*
>
> *In utter despair I reached out at my first Al-Anon meeting, and a room full of people grasped me, lifted me up and gave me hope, love and faith. . . . They explained the disease . . . and best of all taught me detachment. . . . Then came the pink cloud of my husband's intensified AA activity and participation. This was his way of holding on to sobriety. We hardly saw him. But I was neither lonely nor neglected; I was participating in my own group. I was striving for the same serenity he was. . . .[1]*

Nar-Anon member:

> *I found this program through the* probation officer *[emphasis added] of a friend of my addict. I didn't have any idea what it was all about but I thought of it as one more avenue of help to investigate. Help for who I wasn't sure. I had heard of Al-Anon and knew that it was for the family but had only a vague idea of its mechanics. When I came I was an emotional wreck. I couldn't make a decision and let it stick but would change it two or three times and then give up in despair and frustration. Each of my days and nights were filled with thoughts of my addict. Full of "whys" and fear and worry and resentment. My first meeting was a soothing balm to my troubled mind and heart.[2]*

This quote could just as well have been that of an addict or alcoholic talking about his or her early exposure to recovery. The pain, the confusion, and the powerlessness associated with out-of-control addiction *is no different* for the nonaddict (or nonalcoholic) loved one or family member. Many experts agree that it is just as important for the concerned family member or loved one to pursue treatment alternatives and/or Twelve Step involvement as it is for the addict.

---

1. Al-Anon Family Groups, "Alcoholism—The Family Disease" (New York: Al-Anon Family Groups, 1972), 8.
2. Nar-Anon Family Groups' pamphlet, *Personal Stories,* 5.

On the surface, this doesn't seem to make sense. They are not the ones using, destroying their lives with substances, or getting in trouble with the law. In fact, the non-chemically addicted family member is usually *the* one person holding the family together, paying the bills, protecting the so-called integrity of the family "system," being accountable to others in the community, and seeing to it that catastrophe is not around the corner. And in that very obsessive and purposeful effort to ensure the family's survival at all cost, they drive themselves (and perhaps others) crazy.

To make an analogy, we can look at it this way: *the addict is to the family member what the alcohol [or drug] is to the alcoholic [or addict].* It's a simple concept, but hard to grasp for most of us. Family members who try to *control* their loved one's drinking or drugging not only make life miserable and unmanageable, but they also wind up unwittingly perpetuating the very condition they wish to eradicate—their loved one's addiction. They do this by enabling; by covering up, making excuses for the addict, cleaning up after the addict, and otherwise ensuring that everything looks okay, on the outside.

These dynamics are very real and repeatedly confound our work with the addicted offender leading up to, during, and after the "intervention" designed to confront his or her substance dependence. Here is the bottom line in virtually all but a few cases: A nonsupportive and/or nonrecovering family system *will* sabotage our best efforts to bring an offender near the brink of change. Expect and prepare for it.

Consequently, it is critical that we conceptualize the family as a system, as a significant force with very real but obviously unwritten "Rules of Engagement." [3] These rules underscore the depths to which the addicted family will go to thwart outside intervention and maintain equilibrium. A typical nonrecovering family system will abide by the following rules:

THE FAMILY SYSTEM'S **RULES OF ENGAGEMENT**

1. The entire family has an *obsession* around offender's use of substances.
2. Everyone in the family believes that the addict *is not really the cause* of the family's problems.

3. As adapted from Sharon Wegscheider, *Another Chance: Hope and Health for the Alcoholic Family* (Palo Alto, Calif.: Science Behavior Books, 1981).

3. Someone else, or something else, really caused the problems in the family (the defense mechanisms of blaming and projection are common within this context).

4. They must maintain the status quo at all costs to ensure the family's survival.

5. Most family members become enablers and therefore unwittingly help perpetuate the addict's problems, allowing him or her to continue to abuse.

6. The addiction is a family secret, and generally should not be discussed inside or outside the family.

7. No one is to speak out; no one is to really say what they are feeling inside.

According to Al-Anon, the rules are clear: *Don't talk, don't feel.* Reflect on our own experiences with families of offenders in trouble with alcohol or drugs. Can we identify some of these rules in operation? Think about circumstances when we may have tried (assuming we had the time to try anything with a family member!) to educate and/or explain why a non-chemically dependent sibling, spouse, or "significant other" needed to confront *his or her* own addictive disease. Remember the cold stare; the empty and uncomfortable silence; or the outright defensiveness? Most of us were met with palpable denial and resistance, the likes of which we assumed were peculiar only to the addict.

Here are some fairly typical nonrecovering family member comments that we might hear, both *before* and *after* an offender's exposure to treatment.

Before Treatment . . .

- "John didn't use all that much, really. Besides, his job was giving him a lot of stress."

- "He drinks a little too much on occasion, but I'm sure he doesn't get into any illegal stuff. Not in this family. No way. He wasn't brought up that way and he knows better."

Before Treatment . . .

- "Well, he's working finally. I don't see why you're so concerned about one or two positive urines. We all make mistakes. We're human, you know."

- "Oh yes, since probation, John is doing so much better. Does he still drink? No. Well, maybe a few beers now and again . . . but that's not really drinking; it's much less than before and never when he drives. I make sure of that!"

- "Look, all of his friends use on weekends and the entire neighborhood is infested with drugs. . . . What do you expect? He's not out of control, as they say; he works and is good to me and the kids. He's what I call 'recreational' about it. You know what the real problem is, though? It's his friends."

After Treatment . . .

- "I make sure John gets to those meetings; I take him myself most of the time. And I closely monitor and stay on him about his friends and 'associates.'"

- "Why does John have to go to so many of those meetings? He's around the house less now than he was before treatment."

- "John wants me to not drink around him. That's not right. I don't have the problem. He's got to learn to handle his habit on his own."

- "John may be 'clean and sober,' as they say, but he is still driving me crazy. He hasn't spent any more time with the kids. He hasn't been any better with his money. He hasn't spent any more time with me. He's still a pain."

After Treatment . . .

- "Oh yeah, we're so proud of John. Three months clean from drugs! We went out to his favorite club and celebrated with champagne, just a little. I knew he could cure his habit."

By adhering as best they can to the "rules of engagement," a family system (or even a couple in this conceptual framework) remains homeostatic, or stable and unchanged. The social scientists remind us that homeostasis is just as important a family dynamic as it is a reality of physical science. When one individual changes or moves in a particular direction, such as by wanting to stop using, it will have a rippling effect on the rest of the family. Initially, it will not be pleasant. Change is difficult. To the already dysfunctional family, the family struggling with addiction, change is particularly threatening, because it throws off their delicate balance.

The "rewards" experienced by a nonrecovering family member perpetuate the offender's addiction. For example, in the case of the typical alcoholic marriage, the nonalcoholic spouse can ensure the continuation of the marriage as long as the alcoholic continues to drink: The drinking spouse *needs* the enabler in order to survive. Simple as that. Abstinence would result in a complete switch in the balance of power and thereby threaten the marriage itself.

Although the non-chemically addicted family member or loved one is usually not aware of it, and would be loathe to admit it *prior to his or her own recovery,* there is significant power available in this control-oriented family paradigm. The control is both obvious and yet subtle. To fear someone's recovery or abstinence (and thereby unwittingly sabotage it) because of an unknown power shift likely to unfold is not something anyone would easily admit. So there are powerful and sometimes fairly well camouflaged secondary rewards for perpetuation of the family system's status quo.

To many, the admission that one's spouse, or lover, or brother, or close friend may be drug or alcohol dependent is tantamount to an admission of complete defeat and shameful despair: *How could this be? Not in our family.* And sometimes admitting that a loved one has a serious problem will trigger thoughts or questions about one's own potential culpability in the process. The question that all spouses or loved ones avoid like the plague comes crashing down: *What must be wrong with me that I got involved with someone like that in the first place?*

Coming to terms with the answer to this question will often precipitate the non-chemically addicted spouse's emotional "bottom," the point when he or she realizes the full ramification of addiction as a family disease, and not solely an individual challenge. Unfortunately, and sadly, there is often very little accurate information on hand about what to do once confronted with either the reality of a family member's addiction or that of one's own co-addiction. Remember: The family member is *almost always* just as uninformed about addiction as the actively addicted offender.

The addict's chances for recovery will be much improved if the family is involved in a Twelve Step or self-help group recovery process—if not so they can engage in recovery, then at least so they gain a greater appreciation of what to expect for their addicted loved one facing this new and threatening world of abstinence.

Al-Anon: Common Misconceptions

Membership Requirements

Al-Anon, as mentioned earlier, is AA's partner fellowship. As such, it will be the primary reference point for this chapter. Al-Anon's early emphasis was very much on how to keep a marriage alive, how to support the doting and enabling wife now that her husband was sober. Members of Al-Anon were almost exclusively wives of recovering alcoholics active in AA.

This is not so today. Although Al-Anon is still predominantly female (88 percent), this may be changing. Generally speaking, there are enough men who find help within their meeting rooms not to make the newcoming male too uncomfortable. Half of Al-Anon's present-day membership, believed to be well over the 500,000 range, have had some college education; most are employed; and more than a quarter are in executive, professional, and managerial positions.

The only requirement for membership in Al-Anon is that an important person in your life is or was troubled by alcohol. The person does not have to be in AA. The person does not have to be in recovery. The person may still be drinking and have no interest in abstinence. The person could be your employer, your lover, your spouse, your best friend, your father, your mother, or your sibling. It does not matter. Half of all members in Al-Anon report being children of alcoholics.

Al-Anon's Purpose

An Al-Anon newcomer will quickly learn they are not there to *get* the alcoholic sober or straight. In Al-Anon, members learn about the disease of alcoholism and how it has adversely affected *them* as well as loved ones. They come for support themselves, not to support the addicted person. They learn about their own self-righteousness, arrogance, anger, denial, and resentment. Many will have to experience an emotional bottom, come to terms with their emotional obsessiveness and controlling ways, and *then* ask for help from others. Without exception, however, newcomers to Al-Anon will arrive with the fantasy that somehow they can get their loved one sober, if only he or she would listen to reason.

Al-Anon cleverly shifts the focus back to self. Members come to realize that once the alcoholic is sober, the problems within an alcoholic family do not miraculously disappear. Sobriety is not the magic pill or panacea for a family's struggle with the disease of addiction. For many, it is but the beginning. Members are there to support one another and to learn from others who have gone before them about how to grow themselves, how not to become entrapped by the disease of addiction, how to put up appropriate boundaries and set limits, and how to concentrate on their own emotional sobriety, as opposed to the more natural tendency to obsess about the alcoholic (sober or not) in their life.

What Al-Anon Is and Is Not

Just like AA, NA, and other Twelve Step-oriented self-help groups, particularly those patterned after AA, Al-Anon is not a professional association; nor is it a religious organization. It is spiritually centered. The Al-Anon Twelve Steps are nearly identical to those of AA. Al-Anon cooperates extensively with the community but adheres to its own version of the Twelve Traditions as means of providing guidelines for its long-term survival. Al-Anon is an independent fellowship that neither endorses nor expresses opinions on outside issues. And finally, there are no dues or fees. Membership is entirely voluntary.

One currently active Al-Anon member put it like this: "Generally, this entire handbook *Partners in Change* is filled with Al-Anon information. . . . Simply substitute the phrase 'family member' or 'loved one' for 'alcoholic' or 'addict.'"

The concept of detachment coupled with the phrase "letting go" are central themes that run throughout the Al-Anon program. Detachment does not mean coldness or indifference to the alcoholic. It does not mean turning away from a loved one and not caring about him or her, or self-righteously dismissing the addict in some way. No, it means "detaching with love." It means coming to accept the idea that by "letting go" and not trying to control another human being, one has the capacity to stay sane and ultimately, effect, far greater change in the long run. By detaching in this way, one is reminded of the Serenity Prayer; that there are indeed things (and people) we cannot change. Topping the list are other people, including one's addicted spouse, lover, parent, or dear friend. Al-Anon members learn how to stop fixing things for the alcoholic, how not to interfere with the natural consequences of their drinking, and how to step back just far enough to accept their own powerlessness over the situation.

The Newcomer Asks

Here are some typical questions that might be posed by a family member prior to an Al-Anon (or Nar-Anon) referral. Within the context of each, we will propose a variety of responses. The focus will be mostly on a general theme; laying out specific or pat answers is usually ineffective. Our role is not to be sponsor or confidant. We are there on behalf of the offender to refer the spouse (or family member) and perhaps provide some education about the addictive disease and recovery process. So we learn what we need to learn about the consequences of addiction on the family. We know our stuff and keep learning. And when we find ourselves with the family member, we talk about what we know with confidence. We do not bluff what we don't know. The family member of an addict or alcoholic is just as sensitive to insincerity as the addicted offender. Again, as with AA and NA, one of the best ways to ensure adequate exposure to the family dynamics of addiction is to attend meetings ourselves.

Remember this, if nothing else: In many instances we are going to be talking to a non-chemically dependent and nonrecovering spouse or significant other who may be just as sick as the addicted offender. The absence of an active addiction, conspicuous or otherwise, does *not* mean the family member has cornered the mental health market.

Some mental health experts openly argue that working with the spouse of an alcoholic or drug addict can present more of a clinical challenge than vice versa. At least with the addict, the drug is removed, you establish a period of abstinence, and the results are immediately recognizable. The changes, the behavioral ones in particular, are tangible and reinforcing to both addict and spouse: no more hangovers, no more drunken arguments, more money in the house, more time at home. Learning not to drink or drug "one day at a time" yields immediate positive reinforcement. But imagine trying to learn to detach, to let go, and to stop the obsessive emotional roller coaster "one day at a time." It just is not as easy, one could argue. Here are the typical newcomer questions:

Why should I attend meetings? I'm not the one abusing alcohol or drugs.

No, but this person *is* likely very confused, angry, and upset about what has happened in the family as a direct consequence of someone else's addiction. People in this situation need support from other family members or friends *who have been through the same ordeal*. Why? Because although they have not personally been abusing substances, they have been around someone who has long enough to have gotten seriously hurt, emotionally and otherwise.

More than likely, they *are* suffering from the secondary effects of the disease of addiction. Trying to keep up the secrets, hold on to the lies, and maintain the image of a fine family is a lonely endeavor.

No, individual family members may not be in an abusive relationship with alcohol or drugs themselves, but they are in a loving relationship with someone who is. So if they are interested in being supportive and trying to do the right thing, then they need encouragement to learn as much as they can about the disease of addiction. If they are serious about wanting to really help, the best thing they can do for themselves, as well as the addicted family member, is get to meetings and get involved in a Twelve Step program of their own.

The addicted family member, using or not using, in or out of recovery, is going to be experiencing many, many changes. The best way to keep up with them, to adapt to them, and to cope with them may very well be to make a commitment to *change oneself*. Since people rarely change on their own, putting oneself in the midst of others who are might be just the motivational ticket!

What can a family member do to help the alcoholic get into recovery?

The family member can do very little to help the alcoholic or addict get into recovery. There are books with titles such as *Don't Help* which try to get the point across that trying to "reform" or help the alcoholic or addict is often a losing proposition. In the traditional sense, trying to help in this way translates into words and phrases such as, "taking care of," "enabling," and "protecting." What a family member can do is work hard at changing his or her own attitude. By so doing, and this is done by going to meetings, of course, he or she provides a healthier living environment for the entire family. Often when this happens (because the family is a *system*), it helps the addict eventually recognize his or her problem and seek help.

Should I stop drinking? Or not let him hang out with drinking friends? Should I not serve drinks at home?

It might be advisable, particularly if it makes a difference to the alcoholic or addict. But this is up to the family member; it is a personal decision. After all, the family member is not the one with the biochemical addiction to a substance. Now, if the nonrecovering spouse *resentfully* quits or decides not to serve drinks at home, there may be something else altogether going on.

What about not letting him hang out with his old friends and buddies who drink and drug? First, how realistic is such a plan? Presumably we are talking about an adult, not a child in need of parental boundaries. Second of all, why now all of a sudden? If this family member did indeed have that much control and influence over the addict, wouldn't there have been many previous unsuccessful attempts? Why try it again? One of the trademark themes of addiction is "doing the same thing over and over again, and expecting different results" (e.g., "One beer won't get me drunk this time"). Is this not the same?

Those of us comfortable with our counseling skills and understanding of the basic principles of family addiction will encourage nonaddicted family members to detach, to let go, and to allow the addict the freedom to make his or her own decisions. Encourage them to stop the negative fantasy that there is sufficient power to control anybody, let alone the addict. It has probably never worked in the past. And if this is difficult to grasp (which it will be), it is exactly why they need to be taking care of themselves by meeting and being around others in a similar predicament.

These questions, or variations on them, will arise with some frequency. Our obligation as professionals is *to shift responsibility for action ("action" = family member getting to meetings) to the nonrecovering family member.* The family members' inclination will be to countershift the focus of action (and attention) back to what they think the alcoholic or addict must do vis-à-vis his or her addiction or recovery. Most will prefer to view themselves in a monitoring or supervision role. They are rarely helpful in this sense.

Once he stops drinking or drugging, will our troubles be over?

Absolutely not. And again, this is precisely why a family member must be encouraged to look into Al-Anon or another appropriate companion Twelve Step group. Just because someone stops the active substance use, there is no guarantee that other problems will not surface, or resurface, as the case may be. Perhaps there is an underlying, coexisting pathology or character disorder. Maybe there is depression or dangerously low self-esteem. Perhaps there are sexual problems and barriers to intimacy. Even more potentially confounding, the newly clean and sober offender may initially behave even worse than before he or she stopped using!

Or, on a more positive note, the recovering addict may substitute most of his or her new free time with attendance at Twelve Step meetings, "meetings after the meetings," and service work; he or she is rarely at home now, may start spending time with new friends in the program, starts talking about the "Steps" and reading program literature, and finds himself or herself on the phone a lot with "strange" people—strange to the family member, that is. This can be very unsettling to the spouse or loved one. The family system has suddenly lost its script and has been turned upside down. Marriages frequently fail when one or the other partner remains in denial about the need for change. In this case, of course, the spouse should be encouraged to get to meetings.

Al-Anon "Works" the Twelve Steps

Al-Anon is a great teacher. It sets a safe staging area for the recovery needs of the participating member. It delineates appropriate boundaries between oneself and the alcoholic (active or not). And perhaps best of all, the Fellowship teaches its membership how to view this devastating addictive disease in a way that does not further frustrate, confound, or demoralize its secondary victims. Within this context, the greatest truth that Al-Anon teaches, and perhaps the best way to lead into a brief discussion of Al-Anon's interpretation of the Twelve Steps, is captured by *"The 'Three Cs' of Al-Anon":*

> *I didn't Cause the alcoholism.*
> *I can't Control it.*
> *I can't Cure it.*

Some have suggested there be a fourth "C" in Al-Anon's credo: "But I Can change myself."

Now to the Twelve Steps, the Al-Anon way. *Al-Anon changed only a single word* in adapting the Twelve Steps of AA: in the Twelfth Step, the word *others* is used in place of *alcoholics.* Otherwise, the Steps are "worked" identically to AA.

To further illustrate this point, imagine an active member of AA mistakenly walking into an Al-Anon Step discussion meeting. Notwithstanding the introductions (Al-Anon members say, "My name is _____ and I am a grateful member of Al-Anon"), it would take several minutes before this person realizes he or she is not in an AA meeting! The content of meetings; the types of discussions; the general flavor or atmosphere of the Fellowship itself; and the companionship, sponsorship, and sharing of "experience, strength, and hope" are all there, just as for the recovering alcoholic active in AA. In fact, many AAs attend Al-Anon meetings as part of their recovery program. They are known as "double winners" and often reveal that although AA got them sober, Al-Anon *keeps* them sober.

With but the few exceptions outlined below, Al-Anon's interpretation of the Twelve Steps differs very little from that of AA's original rendition. Let us now review them through the eyes of a typical Al-Anon member. Note their versatility for almost *any* obsession or addiction problem.

Step One

The Al-Anon member comes face to face with his or her utter powerlessness over alcohol, as it manifests itself in the form of *alcoholism.* He or she tries, and tries again, over and over, to control or change the addict's addiction. Each time the results are the same: a humbling admission of being just as out of control and powerless as the "sick and troubled drinker."[4] So as the newcomer to Al-Anon surrenders to the powerfulness of alcoholism and/or addiction (just as the alcoholic must in this Step), a new way of life begins to unfold.

Steps Two and Three

The Al-Anon member is challenged to make another difficult admission: "that the way we have been thinking, acting, and living was not reasonable or sane."[5] Step Two suggests that the Al-Anon member "came to believe" that something greater than self-will, a Higher Power for example, could "restore" his or her family to sanity. Sanity is described in terms of the battle most family members have over deciding who really is out of his or her mind and the craziness associated with living under the same roof as an alcoholic. However, for the Al-Anon member the challenge is to turn around and look within, to admit that one's obsession over someone else's problem has caused pain, self-destruction, and helplessness.

Of course, making the decision to "turn our will and our lives over to the care of God *as we understood Him,*" or taking Step Three, is much simpler when built on the preceding Step. As with the recovering alcoholic, the Al-Anon member works this Step by admitting he or she cannot handle the problem alone and by beginning to trust a Higher Power. It means accepting help and acknowledging the fruitlessness of what the Big Book calls "self-will run riot." Al-Anon acknowledges that thousands and thousands of unhappy people have initially entered their rooms asking but one favor: sobriety for the addict or alcoholic (just as the AA newcomer might initially demand information about how to drink responsibly!).

---

4. *Al-Anon Family Groups,* (New York: Al-Anon Family Group Headquarters, Inc., 1987), 39.
5. *Al-Anon Family Groups,* 40.

Steps Four, Five, and Six

These Steps challenge the member to look squarely in the face of such ugly and uncomfortable character traits as self-pity, resentment, intolerance, self-righteousness, and fearfulness. The family members begin to learn more about their part in the disease process and how to eradicate the sick secrets that typically harbor the active addiction.

Steps Seven, Eight, and Nine

As you recall from chapter 4, these are the Steps of reconciliation. They are virtually indistinguishable when worked either by the AA or Al-Anon member. By "humbly" asking one's Higher Power to take away the shortcomings (i.e., those character defects that were discovered during the self-examination in Step Four) that stand in the way of achieving a sense of purposefulness and serenity, a person moves on, examines important relationships in his or her life (past and present), and finally puts the past to rest by making "direct amends," where necessary.

Steps Ten, Eleven, and Twelve

Now for the "final Three," known in *both* AA and Al-Anon, as the "maintenance Steps." The continuing self-evaluation or daily inventory suggested in Step Ten is just as important for the nonaddicted family member as it is for the alcoholic. What happens when the family member slips back into old habits like nagging, complaining, directing, self-righteousness, and overcontrolling behavior, *regardless of whether or not the addict or alcoholic has stopped using?* More obsession over the alcoholic or addict; less serenity for the family member.

The seriously motivated Al-Anon member, in the context of the Eleventh Step, is just as intrigued about the prospect of developing meditative skills and a consequent sense of spirituality (not religion) as is the recovering addict or alcoholic at this same juncture in his or her journey. The Twelfth Step emphasis on helping, on getting out of oneself and "passing it on," as exemplified by the oft-quoted AA saying, "You can't keep it unless you give it away," is just as strong in Al-Anon as in AA. Sponsorship and networking with others in the Fellowship are also important facets of Al-Anon.

Nar-Anon Family Groups: Still Growing

Nar-Anon, as mentioned earlier, is the partner or companion fellowship of Narcotics Anonymous. It is designed for relatives and other loved ones of someone who has an addiction. Usually, members are relatives or close friends of men and women who are not primarily alcoholic and have a history of abusing illegal substances such as narcotics, speed, marijuana, or other such black-market drugs. They, too, stress the importance of concentrating on themselves, and not the addict in their life. By so doing, some members find answers to many of life's problems, many of which are completely unassociated with addiction.

Most, if not all, of the aforementioned information about Al-Anon comfortably applies to Nar-Anon as well. Nar-Anon began in the early 1970s and was closely patterned after Al-Anon. In terms of a comparative description, it is safe to say that *Nar-Anon is as different from Al-Anon as NA is from AA.* Unfortunately, it is not nearly as widely known or available as Al-Anon. Its overall membership is also much smaller. However, it is out there, more predominant in urban areas and larger cities. Probation officers may have to search a little harder to find directories and meetings that have survived over some period of time. Do not give up. We can be a valuable referral source for Nar-Anon as it works toward building its membership ranks.

All of the "Do's and Don'ts" described below also apply to utilizing Nar-Anon as a companion community resource. As with most other referrals, but especially with Nar-Anon since it is younger and less widespread, we should devote some time to looking into availability of meetings and what the general atmosphere is for them in a particular geographic location. Try not to stop there. Go to several open meetings, introduce yourself, and start an informal community liaison with group members. By so doing, you not only avail yourself of the latest directories or lists of meetings (some of which might be brand-new and not even formally listed), but you may also come away with valuable insights about making choices between sending someone to Nar-Anon or Al-Anon, or both! As with NA and AA, in Nar-Anon and Al-Anon there is an overlapping phenomenon: members fluctuate between one or the other, or experience both and then make a decision as to which feels more comfortable.

Community Supervision Techniques

In the spirit of efficiency and "keeping it simple," remember that families, close friends, and loved ones of the addicted offender need introduction to Al-Anon or Nar-Anon for three main reasons:

1. So that they may begin to understand what addiction and recovery are all about.

2. So that the addicted offender is less likely to experience family sabotage or enabling.

3. So that when a lot of unanticipated change is experienced by the family member of a loved one as a consequence of the recovery process, they are not overwhelmed.

In the ideal world, we will play an active role in introducing family members to these companion Twelve Step support groups. We cannot mandate attendance, but we can encourage, refer, and re-refer. Bringing the family together as part of an intervention "team" increases the likelihood of a positive response on the part of the addicted offender. Here are some general guidelines that help us in working with a family member or loved one.

- **Do** *ask, each and every time a family member calls (and they* will *call) to talk about, complain about, and ask about the addict, "Have you been to any support-group [Al-Anon or Nar-Anon, as the case may be] meetings yet?"*

- **Don't** *get caught up in the battle over why they (family members) should be going to meetings ("I'm not the one with the problem");* simply advise them that in order to understand what is going on with the addict, they must interact with and be around others who have been there. Nothing more, nothing less. Avoid pointing out why they may need help.

- **Do** *routinely ask family members the following question, particularly ones who have had some introductory exposure to Al-Anon or Nar-Anon and who persist in complaining about their circumstances, or trying to gain your commiserative allegiance: "Have you found a sponsor yet?" or "Do you have a sponsor?"*

- **Don't** *act like or become a surrogate sponsor for a family member or loved one of the addicted offender.* We are community corrections professionals, not "friends." We are not equipped with the objectivity or professional detachment necessary for rendering that type of assistance.

- **Do** *tell the family members or loved ones that even if the addict is still using, they can and* should *look into attending meetings themselves.*

- **Do** *tell the family members or loved ones that even if the addict is clean and sober, they can and* should *look into attending meetings themselves.*

- **Don't** *let the family member, or loved one, or even employer tell you that the addicted offender cannot attend meetings because of other responsibilities.* Nothing should get in the way of attendance at meetings. The person who makes such an excuse should be immediately referred to Al-Anon or Nar-Anon.

- ***Don't*** *hesitate to refer families with children to either Alateen or Narateen groups.* A part of Al-Anon Family Groups, Alateen is a fellowship of young people whose lives have been affected by alcoholism in a family member or close friend.

- ***Do*** *tell the family member that it is the addict's responsibility to call or otherwise provide information to the probation officer about why he or she cannot attend a meeting, a counseling session, or some other aftercare commitment.*

- ***Don't*** *allow the family member to be the primary source of information or messages between you and the offender.* You can become just as much an *enabler* as the family member.

- ***Don't*** *condone family members' or loved ones' inclination to chaperone the addict to his or her meetings.* This is not their purpose or business. They should be going to their *own* Twelve Step meetings if they really want to "help."

- ***Do*** *keep an updated listing of companion Twelve Step meetings in your office or your car (especially if you do a lot of field work, because this is where you will encounter the most family members) right next to the AA/NA resources.*

- ***Do*** *attend meetings yourself!* Although Al-Anon and Nar-Anon are specifically for the family and friends of alcoholics or addicts, community corrections workers can and *should* attend open speakers meetings to get a good flavor of what it is all about. It is also an excellent place to pick up literature for the office.

Notes on Postresidential Treatment

For most of us in community corrections, the biggest frustration in working with the addicted offender comes not in the beginning, during the confrontation or intervention stage, but further down the line, following detox or after a period of residential treatment when it is time to go home. Returning to the neighborhood, the comfortable streets, the dysfunctional family, and all the old friends does very little in most cases to sustain the commitment to stay in recovery.

The breakdown is very real. At first it may be subtle and very unconscious. Remember that relapse *rarely,* if ever, starts with the first drink or drug. It starts much earlier, sometimes weeks or months earlier, with cognitive distortion, "stinking thinking," or emotional conflict and frustration that may lead to bad decisions. Take a look at the following three scenarios, which are meant to illustrate what typically happens to many offenders just out of treatment.

On Going Home: Prescription for Relapse?

Example 1

Lamont exercises an innocent choice to stop off and pay a quick visit to an old street corner, "just to let the guys know I'm cool, that I'm now about getting my life together." He stays in the same neighborhood, sees the same hangouts, passes by the same clubs and liquor stores, and tries to convince himself that he can do all this by exercising his willpower not to get high. After all, he now knows he is an addict and CAN'T. But he "is not about" trying to really make the total switch . . . to an abstinent and positive lifestyle.

He wants to try and live in both worlds, the familiar streets and conventional society. He is convinced that he is powerful enough to live this double life. He'll have a couple of token NA or AA friends, but most of his buddies will remain steeped in the negative environment. He is able to pull it off for a while. But time begins to challenge him. As AA and NA say, "If you hang around a barber shop long enough, you'll eventually get a haircut." Lamont doesn't pull it off; he relapses and the cycle starts all over again. But this time his parole officer must take him off the streets in the name of therapeutic accountability.

Example 2

John lives alone now. He has been out of a twenty-eight-day inpatient treatment program for one week. One day he decides to visit his ex-wife and children on the way home from work. After all, this is the right thing to do: to show responsibility and spend time with his kids. He exercises this choice even though he knows she is an active addict, will probably be high, and in the past has always tried to get him to party with her. The initial motivation is clean. The underlying motivation is not. It is driven by the chemical dependency, even though that dependency is temporarily in remission. John may be able to hold on and not get high this time. He may not be so lucky the next time his addiction decides to alter his route.

Example 3

Tom returns home from what he freely described as a very "positive" ninety-day residential treatment experience. He is sincere about staying clean and sober, attending meetings, and keeping his counseling appointments. His attitude is strong. He says all the right things to both his counselor and probation officer.

But then he has to face his neighborhood and the inevitable relapse triggers. Even worse is what goes on inside his own home. Nothing has changed there since his probation officer directed him into inpatient treatment ninety days ago. Drug-dependent siblings continue to get high and abuse alcohol. Dad is out of the picture, and Mom is drinking heavily to medicate her pain. He hears the music, smells the marijuana, and feels the family resentment the moment he walks through the door. There is no support. No one really understands what he is trying to do with his life, let alone understand the principles of recovery. Relapse eventually becomes a comfortable relief.

So for many addicted offenders (not all, by any means) who are serious about their recovery, a return to the same neighborhood, family, or negative environment in general will be tantamount to initiating the relapse process. Not right away, necessarily, but eventually; once the "pink cloud" wears off, once being clean for a period of time loses its novelty. Note that this is a distinct possibility *even if the offender is sincere and diligent in his or her Twelve Step meeting attendance.* The pull, the power, and the influence of negative environmental and social influences can be that devastating.

Oxford House: A Workable "Geographic Cure"

There is an alternative to these negative influences, available in many parts of the country today (and growing!), called Oxford House, Inc. Oxford Houses are self-run, self-supported, multiresident houses (often located in "nicer" neighborhoods) that groups of recovering alcoholics and drug addicts rent "to live together in an environment supportive of recovery from addiction."[6] Each group obtains a charter from Oxford House, Inc., the umbrella organization for the national network of individual Oxford Houses (see appendix A). The first one was started in 1975 in Silver Spring, Maryland. In 1993 there were over 472 Oxford Houses in thirty-five different states. Their goal is to have 10,000 houses by the year 2000!

The conceptual framework is the belief that recovering individuals can help one another change. Sound familiar? Of course it does; it is the identical theoretical—and for that matter, practical—foundation that fuels the success of Twelve Step groups like AA and NA. In their own words, "Oxford House simply expanded the opportunity for individuals to practice the principles of AA and NA by developing a practical way for recovering individuals to live together in a supportive family environment. That 'practical way' is simply to rent a house and to

---

6. Oxford House, Inc. 1992 Annual Report.

live together effectively by following a tested system of operations."[7] Oxford House, Inc., is not affiliated in any way with AA or NA, but they certainly interact and support one another to the best of their abilities.

At the core of the aforementioned "system of operations" are the three basic rules contained in every individual Oxford House charter. These simple rules capture the essence of what Oxford Houses are really all about, how they are run, and why there is every reason to believe they will continue to flourish in the future.

THREE BASIC OXFORD HOUSE RULES

- The house must be democratically self-run.
- The house must be financially self-supported.
- The house must expel any resident who relapses.

The original founders struggled over this problem of what to do with the person who returns to drug or alcohol use while in the house. From the start, they recognized the rule had to be absolute. This rule, incidentally, came from their experience within the county-run halfway houses, where such infractions resulted in immediate expulsion. The problem became how to issue guidelines or procedures to make sure that any resident who drank or took drugs would be thrown out.

Once a member has been expelled, usually determined by the results of a group meeting in which the majority rules, he or she cannot be readmitted unless there is a clear demonstration that he or she has returned to solid sobriety. Each house develops its own set of rules to determine this. Some accept completion of a twenty-eight-day treatment program. Others require at least a month of no drinking or drugging and solid Twelve Step program activity. Once houses have opened up within a particular geographic area, they keep in touch with one another to prevent a relapsing member from moving from one house to another.

Oxford House members are very serious about this tradition or governing rule—so much so, and this is the beauty of peer support, that more often than not, house members are able to pick up on someone's potential for relapse way *before* the drink or drug is ingested. Living day in and day out with other recovering addicts, most, if not all, of whom are active in their respective Twelve Step

---

7. Oxford House, Inc. 1992 Annual Report.

program, lends itself well to spotting the signs and symptoms (e.g., attitude change, irritation, displays of anger, failure to complete chores or attend house meetings) before the drug-taking behavior begins.

The following are typically asked questions about Oxford Houses:

How long can an offender stay in an Oxford House?

People can stay as long as they want, provided they maintain their abstinence and assume an equal share of house expenses. The average length of stay is a little over a year, with many staying as long as three, four, or more years.

How effective are Oxford Houses? Are there outcome studies available?

Very effective, and yes, outcome studies are available. One, conducted in June of 1992 involved a detailed evaluation of twenty different Oxford Houses established in New Jersey. Results showed that 552 individuals had lived in them during the period of time studied (April of 1990 to March of 1992). Of the 552, only 132 had returned to the use of alcohol or drugs—24 percent. The remainder had an average of more than eight months' continuous sobriety. Eighty-six percent of the respondents viewed Oxford House as "very important" to their personal recovery.[8]

What about typical Oxford House demographics?

For the New Jersey study mentioned above, the following statistics were generated and may be of some interest in establishing a demographic profile, at least for the Northeast:

- Forty-one percent had been homeless for six months or more.
- Fifty-six percent had done jail time, averaging one year sixty-two days.
- Sixty-three percent were white; 37 percent were African American.
- More than two-thirds had been through treatment three or more times.
- Almost all were employed at the time of survey.
- The average resident attends over five AA or NA meetings per week.

How much clean or sober time is required for admission to an Oxford House?

There is no minimum amount of clean or sober time. Generally, though, a person is coming after a twenty-eight-day or longer rehabilitation program. Individual houses have their own rules and regulations, of course. Admission

---

8. Oxford House, Inc. 1992 Annual Report.

is granted by an 80 percent vote by the residents. If residents question an applicant's sincerity about his or her "program" or commitment to sobriety, he or she will not be voted in.

What about employment at admission?

Most (but not all) Oxford Houses prefer that applicants be employed at admission. Sometimes a prospective resident will be given the go-ahead to stay for an agreed-upon period of time (two weeks; one month) without bona fide employment, provided he or she is able to come up with an agreed-upon amount for a security deposit at time of admission.

Guidelines for Community Corrections Workers

Oxford House, Inc., is fast becoming one of the most important and cost-free community-based resources available for community corrections. The following guidelines highlight ways in which we must make proper utilization of this valuable companion community resource.

- If it is available within the community, always consider the viability of an Oxford House referral for addicted offenders about to be discharged from long-term treatment facilities.
- We (especially probation officers) should do our utmost to visit with professional treatment staff or counselors while an offender is still in treatment to discuss the option of Oxford House residence (or other sober transitional living arrangements available in the community) as part of an aftercare plan.
- Give consideration to development of an "aftercare contract," signed by the offender during residential treatment, that stipulates he or she will seek Oxford House admission following discharge from treatment.
- Always consider an Oxford House referral for *any* offender willing to add "insurance" to a recovery plan, regardless of whether or not he or she has been referred for professional treatment.
- Do not confuse Oxford Houses with traditional halfway houses run by outside state or county authorities. Resistance by the offender is to be expected. So know your stuff and be ready to refer, re-refer, and re-re-refer.
- Have an established line of communication between either individual Oxford Houses or a local branch office so that you have immediate access to vacancy listings and specific addresses to pass on to the inquiring offender.

- Consider taking a more proactive role in outreach efforts. Think about ways to support the Oxford Houses' goal to grow and flourish so that availability is less of a problem.

- Keep in mind that Oxford Houses are not treatment alternatives or ways to get someone clean. There is no professional treatment, only group support and a "clean" living environment.

Summary

So there you have it: We've examined the importance of a supportive family, peer group, and residential environment in sustaining the recovery process for the addicted offender. Because the effect of the family is often overlooked and misunderstood, we described the family dynamics of addictive disease, including such concepts as enabling and family sabotage. To counter these negative influences, we introduced and described three successful companion community resources available for referrals: Al-Anon, Nar-Anon, and Oxford Houses. The family members and loved ones of the addicted offender found in these groups are the "experts." Use them.

CHAPTER 7

A Collective Response:
Supervision Accountability Revisited

Responding to the Challenge

We began this book with a challenge: How can we better respond to community supervision of the addicted offender? We examined the characteristics of the "addiction problem" and determined its complex and multidimensional nature. We noted that *most* criminal offenders abuse alcohol and drugs. Consequently, those of us working with this population in the community cannot afford to minimize or downplay the significance of this reality: The addiction problem is rapidly becoming synonymous with community corrections in general. It is rare indeed to have one without the other.

Next, we defined our overall mission statement: To carry out specific court or paroling authority directives by modifying or changing offender behavior through strategic behavioral intervention so that we may protect and maintain public safety. Again, these are the parameters within which we must try and manage our respective caseloads, the *majority* of which are going to be in trouble with alcohol and drugs.

Incidentally, there are those who disagree that addicted offenders populate the majority of our caseloads. Sometimes it doesn't appear as such on the surface, but turn over the rock and see what squirms beneath. For example, if probation caseloads were "manageable," say within the twenty- to fifty-person range, depending upon specialization needs, there would be no debate. The administrative distractions and paperwork would slow down, and we would have time to identify the addicted offender. Remember that addiction, by its very nature, seeks to hide, to minimize, or to masquerade as something else altogether. This is no different from the scientific laws governing gravity: drop it and it will fall. And with addiction, have it and it will hide.

We have responded to our challenge by introducing Twelve Step self-help groups as *the* primary vehicle through which to navigate a quagmire of varying philosophical, methodological, and attitudinal biases that seem to predominate the field of community corrections. Chemical dependency treatment remains a mysterious and challenging quest. Research shows promising new information every day. But we are not there yet; we have no pill, no panacea, no cure. As AA and NA members have been known to say about their program, "This is a simple program for complicated people." This is true, especially when we face one of the only known pathological conditions to man that tells its victims they do not have it!

We need not respond to this challenge alone. Going it alone with this population *will* generate burnout, cynicism, and a harmful form of Self-righteous indignation (SRI). We need help. So we turn to those in the community who are the real "experts" on addiction and recovery, the ones who have demonstrated their ability to "stay stopped" and help families: AA, NA, Al-Anon, Nar-Anon, and other Twelve Step-oriented self-help groups.

"Systemic Recovery": An Analogy

Just as the individual offender, caught within the disastrous confines of addictive disease, must come to terms with and accept his or her condition (the First Step) before entering the recovery phase, so too must we, as a system or as individual practitioners, accept *our problem* with the "addiction problem."

We admit that the "problem" exists; that it is multidimensional in nature; that it is not simply a question of "a nice system that occasionally drinks too much." Again, the roots run deep, the etiology of the *systemic* problem is just as complex and multifaceted as the disease itself. We must not look the other way when it comes to addiction. This kind of thinking only serves to perpetuate the problem.

It also means, as discussed in chapter 2, recognizing the importance of looking within and examining our own attitudes and beliefs about addiction (the Fourth Step) *before* we do anything at all. We challenge ourselves to know what we need to know about drugs, alcohol, and addiction in an academic as well as phenomenological perspective, particularly since most of us never experimented. By taking our own inventory (the Tenth Step) as we go along, we see that we cannot educate ourselves or develop the arsenal of tools necessary to work with this population single-handedly. We need the community of people who have done it, who have successfully recovered.

The analogy moves us further toward Twelve Step literacy by stressing the importance of getting comfortable with the Twelve Step groups themselves, the mechanics of meetings, and even the individual Steps and Traditions. We learn that *perfunctory* referrals will not work and that we, too, must grow professionally and expand our skills in the art of Twelve Step referrals. Do we know about and have enough confidence in that to which we refer? Do we take the time to refer, re-refer, and re-re-refer? Do we try our best to work with the resistance? Do we understand where the resistance comes from?

We expect offenders to get to meetings, to alter lifestyles, and to start asking for help. We must do the same by getting to open Twelve Step meetings, by exposing ourselves to the *process of recovery* at work, witnessing the reality of these personal revolutions within the meetings, and thereby enhancing our own reservoirs of hope from which we might draw to "pass on" to offenders.

We begin to realize, as does the recovering person at some point in sobriety, that just expecting an offender not to use is usually not enough. We come to say to the offender, *Abstinence alone is not recovery.* But do we really believe this concept or at least accept its legitimate position as a guiding principle in working with this population? It means talking with offenders about what they are doing differently today that is going to ensure they "stay stopped." It means talking about that old adage "the same person will drink or drug again." Naturally, it also means listening and taking the time to point out faulty thinking ("stinking thinking").

To the offender in the early stages of recovery, one of the most difficult tasks he or she faces is reaching out to the community and asking for help, whether it means asking someone to sponsor him or her, simply getting a ride to a meeting, or moving into an Oxford House for continued support. The tendency is to want to go it alone, to handle it, and to hit a meeting now and then but remain separate from a network within the recovering community.

As a system, we are guilty of this as well. We forget about or fail to enlist the support of our companion resources such as Al-Anon, Nar-Anon, or Oxford House, Inc. Or we prefer to remain within our own "programming" mode and not consider new and creative ways of accessing available community resources. Some of us fall prey to our own grandiosity and think that if we just counsel the person enough he or she will eventually "get it" and make positive changes. Not always, for this brand of enabling leads only to burnout and relapse.

The system is stressed out and overburdened. Most of us have unreasonably high caseloads. We work hard just to keep up with offender contacts, reporting re-arrests, managing violations, and meeting the demands of our administrative responsibilities. So unlike the typical denial system manifested by offenders when they point to everything but themselves in either explaining away or rationalizing their disease, we do have very real external circumstances and restraints (policy, economics, the political climate, and so on) that end up inhibiting the full range of our response potential. But despite this distinction we must persevere.

So we see that both as a system and as individual criminal justice professionals within the system, we must undergo many of the same remarkable *internal* changes (whether they be political, economic, personal, or professional) that face the addicted offender standing on the brink of his or her much more limited field of options: treatment, jail, or death. By working hard toward Twelve Step literacy we discover the viability of a *collective* response to the original challenge. And in so doing, our mission becomes more realistic and we become more accountable to it.

We learn that by working as a team we produce results: positive intervention and behavioral change. The influence might not be immediate, or at the moment of referral, but perhaps much later when the offender "gets sick and tired of being sick and tired," as they say in AA. Our greatest measure of success may remain totally unobserved: the probation or parole "failures" who return to AA or NA at a later date, years following the expiration of their case, knowing of no other place to turn for help. At least they now know.

Final Thoughts: Toward a New Paradigm

The American criminal justice system has recently experienced a growing preoccupation with supervision accountability and offender compliance. Some call it the "new penology." Community protection and "zero-tolerance" mandates occasionally assume precedence over traditional counseling and rehabilitative ideals. Within this atmosphere it is not unusual for the results of a single urinalysis report to render all that is necessary to "dispose" of a case without regard to individual circumstances or subsequent evaluation. A "positive for cocaine" could automatically mean revocation and loss of freedom.

Such knee-jerk reactions have several pitfalls, not the least of which is a complete disregard for the individual offender, the prognosis for his or her particular drug problem, the relapse phenomenon, and an appropriate individualized treatment plan. We owe it to ourselves as professionals, as well as to offenders, to move beyond this simplistic, reactionary response. Supervision accountability, individual assessment, and a meaningful relationship with the offender are not mutually exclusive facets of our role in community corrections.

In fact, a firm but consistently applied "empathic supervision" style that focuses on assessment and relationship formation will ensure much tighter and long-lasting accountability standards. Research need not substantiate this point. It is common sense, albeit paradoxical.

Empathic supervision demands that we work toward development of a relationship with the offender that approximates elements of trust and respect. It is *not* a two-way street for obvious reasons of community protection. However, unless the offender respects us as professionals (which leads eventually to trust), the game is over before it begins. Empathy is not a term casually embraced by criminal justice professionals today. Somehow it sounds like *social work* or *treatment,* words that presumably diminish the fundamental law-enforcement philosophy. Nevertheless, in reality they need not be such strange bedfellows.

Empathic supervision simply means placing emphasis on getting to know individual offenders and understanding their predicament, from their perspective. In more concrete terms, it means playing an active role in their recovery, both before and after referral. It means spending time listening, asking the right questions, conveying respect, reinforcing achievement, and continually assessing the person's commitment to recovery. The end result will be more information, enhanced accountability (or law enforcement), and certainly more effective supervision.

A Compendium of Mutual Support Groups
(National, Local, Twelve Step, and Other Models)[1]

Introduction

The following compendium of self-help support groups, called "mutual-support" groups by some, will not be limited to those patterned after the Twelve Steps of AA. Groups that are known to be Twelve Step-oriented will be so noted. Groups that are not, or ones that have become known as alternatives to the traditional Twelve Step model, will also be highlighted. We have limited the compilation to groups that have some common relationship to or involvement with the problem of addiction. We will primarily list national groups that have many chapters. A few "model" groups will be noted; they are local and have only one chapter. Readers are encouraged to contact these groups for educational materials, information on local meetings, and assistance on how to start or develop a group of their own.

Mutual support groups are self-governing, generally voluntary (we use that term loosely in this context, of course) groups of people who come together to face a common problem or life situation. They join forces and share support, encouragement, and practical techniques for overcoming or learning to live with the particular problem. Formats will vary. Some will be Twelve Step-oriented and others will not, but generally there will be sharing of information, pooling of experiential knowledge, opportunities for questions and answers, and significant outside resource availability through contacts developed within. Most have developed, like AA and NA, a combination of educational (speakers meetings) and discussion formats. Unlike AA and NA, some groups that are not Twelve Step-based choose to have experts and professionals serve as guest speakers, facilitators, or

---

1. Adapted from *Directory of Self-Help Support Groups,* published in 1993 by the Mental Health Association of Northern Virginia, 7630 Little River Turnpike, Suite 206, Annandale, Va. 22003; (703) 941-LINK.

medical advisors at the request of the group. It would be safe to say that a common underlying theme uniting all of them is a fundamental philosophy of acceptance and unconditional support. According to one self-help group "clearinghouse," mutual-support groups exist for almost every type of human condition, concern, or life situation. Some estimate that more than 500,000 groups operate in the United States alone, with over fifteen million total participants. It is cautioned, as was underscored several times within the book, that these groups are *not* professional; they are not meant to take the place of trained health care services. They simply recognize the tremendous impact of peer support in confronting and overcoming personal challenges of all types. Working in tandem with traditional (and professionally based) health care, there is real opportunity for change.

Group Listings

Academics Recovering Together (ART)

- National Network
- Founded 1989

Multipurpose, informal network for academic professionals in recovery from alcohol and drug addiction; exchanges information for professionals interested in sabbaticals, relocation, and issues surrounding promotion and tenure.

> **Contact:** Bruce Donovan, Brown University, Box 1865, Providence, RI 02912. Call (401) 863-3831.

Adult Children of Alcoholics (ACA or ACOA)

- World Service Organization; International
- Founded 1976

Twelve Step program of discovery and recovery for adults who were raised in an alcoholic home and who come to realize that "characteristics which allowed them to survive as children in an alcoholic dysfunctional home now prevent them from fully experiencing life."[2]

> **Note:** Going to both AA or NA (or another Twelve Step program) *and* ACA or ACOA meetings is often not recommended for persons early (within the first year) in their own recovery. Get a professional assessment first. Given the powerful emotional content of some ACA meetings, a person could be at greater risk for relapse. **Contact:** ACA, P.O. Box 3216, Torrance, CA 90510. Call (310) 534-1815.

---

2. *Directory of Self-Help Support Groups.*

Al-Anon Family Groups

- International
- Founded 1951

Twelve Step-based program of men, women, children, and adult children whose lives have been affected by the compulsive drinking of a family member or friend. Second only to AA in size and widespread availability. See chapter 6 for a full description of this fellowship and how it helps its participants overcome the ravages of addictive disease from the family perspective.

> **Contact:** Al-Anon Family Groups, P.O. Box 862, Midtown Station, New York, NY 10018-6106. Call (212) 302-7240 (NY) or (800) 344-2666 (meeting information) or (800) 356-9996 (general information). Can sometimes find listings in local telephone book.

Alateen/Ala-Preteen/Alatot

- International
- Founded 1957

Twelve Step-oriented fellowship of young Al-Anon members, usually teenagers, whose lives have been affected by someone else's drinking. Adult members of Al-Anon serve as sponsors for each group.

> **Contact:** Alateen, P.O. Box 862, Midtown Station, New York, NY 10018-0862. Call (212) 302-7240 or (800) 344-2666.

Alcoholics Anonymous World Services, Inc.

- International
- Founded 1935

The premier Twelve Step fellowship for people to share their experience, strength, and hope with each other to solve their common problem of alcoholism and to help others achieve sobriety. Local AA "desk" or "office" for information about meeting availability (including transportation to and from if requested, such as for someone in town on business) is typically listed in the phone book. For comprehensive literature, catalogues, starter packets, domestic and international directories, and information on professional community interaction with the program, see contact address below.

> **Contact:** General Service Office, AA World Services, Inc., 475 Riverside Dr., 11th Floor, New York, NY 10115. Call (212) 870-3400.

Augustine Fellowship, Sex and Love Addicts Anonymous

- International
- Founded 1976

Twelve Step fellowship for those who desire to stop living out a pattern of sex and love addiction, obsessive or compulsive sexual behavior, or emotional attachment.

> **Contact:** P.O. Box 119, New Town Branch, Boston, MA 02258. Call (617) 332-1845.

Black Women in Recovery

- Model
- Founded 1990

Mutual support for recovering women who share their experience, strength, and hope with each other in helping to maintain a positive, chemical-free lifestyle. They have a newsletter, phone support, conferences, pen pals, and meetings. Availability is limited.

> **Contact:** P.O. Box 19003, Lansing, MI 48901-9003. Call (517) 543-0084.

Calix Society

- National
- Founded 1947

Twelve Step-oriented groups of Catholic alcoholics maintaining their sobriety through Alcoholics Anonymous. They are largely concerned with total abstinence, spiritual development, and sanctification of the whole personality of each member. Have bi-monthly newsletter and will provide assistance in chapter development.

> **Contact:** Rolf Olson, 7601 Wayzata Blvd., Minneapolis, MN 55426. Call (612) 546-0544 (mornings only).

Chapter Nine Group of Hollywood

- Model
- Founded 1989

Twelve Step program of recovering couples (addictions/substance abuse) in which partners work together to share their experience, strength, and hope with each other as couples to maintain a positive and chemical-free lifestyle. Group name comes from chapter 9 of the AA "Big Book," *Alcoholics Anonymous,* based on the belief that members of the family or couples should meet upon the common ground of "tolerance, understanding, and love."

Contact: Don Justice, 1168 White Sands Dr., Lusby, MD 20657. Call (301) 586-1425.

Chemically Dependent Anonymous (CDA)

- Model
- Founded 1980

Purpose is to carry the message of recovery to the chemically dependent person (drugs, alcohol, or both). Information, referrals, phone support, conferences, and group development guidelines available.

Contact: P.O. Box 423, Severna Park, MD 21146. Call (301) 647-7060.

Clergy Serving Clergy

- Model
- Founded 1987

Volunteer group of recovering clergy giving help and support to one another. They assist in the identification, early intervention, proper treatment, and productive recovery from the abuse of alcohol or other chemicals by clergy and family members. Quarterly newsletter available.

Contact: 3509 Dana Dr., Burnsville, MN 55337. Call (612) 894-4582.

Co-Anon Family Groups

- International
- Founded 1985

A Twelve Step program for friends and family of people who have problems with cocaine or drugs.

Contact: P.O. Box 64742-66, Los Angeles, CA 90064; call (714) 647-6698; or for East Coast information, contact: P.O. Box 1080 Cooper Station, New York, NY 10276-1080. Call (212) 713-5133.

Cocaine Anonymous

- International
- Founded 1982

Fellowship of men and women who share their experience, strength, and hope that they may solve their common problem (primarily with cocaine) and help others to recover from addiction. Many cocaine addicts prefer involvement in this program as their primary resource with NA as a supplemental group. Fashions itself on Twelve Step model.

> **Contact:** 3740 Overland Ave., #H, Los Angeles, CA 90034. Call (800) 347-8998 (24 hours; meeting information) or (310) 559-5833 (business office).

Co-Dependents Anonymous

- International
- Founded 1986

Fellowship of men, women, and teens whose common problem is an inability to maintain functional relationships. Members desire healthy, fulfilling relationships with others and themselves. Follows the Twelve Step program adapted from AA.

> **Contact:** P.O. Box 3357, Phoenix, AZ 85067-3577. Call (602) 277-7991.

Co-Dependents Anonymous for Helping Professionals (CODAHP)

- International
- Founded 1985

Twelve Step group for professionals working in human services who are in recovery from codependency issues.

> **Contact:** P.O. Box 42253, Mesa, AZ 85212. Call (602) 468-1149.

Co-Dependents of Sex Addicts

- National

A self-help program of recovery using the Twelve Steps adapted from AA and Al-Anon, for those involved in relationships with people who have compulsive sexual behavior. Provides assistance in starting new groups.

> **Contact:** P.O. Box 14537, Minneapolis, MN 55414. Call (612) 537-6904.

Co-Sex and Love Addicts Anonymous

- International
- Founded 1989

Fellowship of relatives, friends, and significant others interested in sharing their experience, strength, and hope in order to find solutions to the problems of dealing with codependent sex and love addiction.

Contact: P.O. Box 614, Brookline, MA 02146-9998.

Debtors Anonymous General Services Board

- National
- Founded 1976

Fellowship that follows the Twelve Step program for mutual help in recovering from compulsive indebtedness. Primary purpose of members is to stay solvent and help other compulsive debtors achieve solvency.

Contact: P.O. Box 400 Grand Central Station, New York, NY 10163-0400. Call (212) 642-8222 (recorded message); (212) 642-8220 (leave a message).

Dentists Concerned for Dentists

- Regional
- Founded 1978

Assists dentists in the recovery from alcoholism or chemical dependency, and other problems such as family, marital, mental health, and financial issues. They have group development guidelines.

Contact: 450 N. Syndicate, #117, St. Paul, MN 55104. Call (612) 641-0730.

Drugs Anonymous

- National

Founded on the suggested Twelve Steps of recovery from addiction, this fellowship is focused on those who want to help themselves and others recover from chemical addiction in general.

Contact: Call (212) 874-0700.

Dual Disorders Anonymous

- Model
- Founded 1982

Twelve Step-oriented fellowship of men and women who come together to help those members who suffer from both a mental disorder and alcoholism and/or drug addiction. Group development guidelines available.

Contact: P.O. Box 4045, Des Plaines, IL 60016. Call (708) 462-3380.

Families Anonymous

- National
- Founded 1971

Mutual support for relatives and friends concerned about the use of drugs or related behavioral problems. Based on the Twelve Step program adopted from AA.

Contact: P.O. Box 528, Van Nuys, CA 91408. Call (818) 989-7841 or (800) 736-9805.

Food Addicts Anonymous

- National
- Founded 1987

A fellowship of men and women who are willing to recover from the disease of food addiction. Primary purpose is to maintain abstinence from sugar, flour, and wheat. Follows Twelve Step program. Provides information and referral, pen pal, conferences, and assistance in starting groups.

Contact: P.O. Box 057394, West Palm Beach, FL 33405-7394.

Gam-Anon Family Groups

- International
- Founded 1960

Provides help for family members and friends of compulsive gamblers by offering Twelve Step-oriented comfort, hope, and friendship through shared experiences. Newsletter, Gam-a-teen groups for teens, group development guidelines, and literature available.

Contact: P.O. Box 157, Whitestone, NY 11357. Call (718) 352-1671.

Gamblers Anonymous

- International
- Founded 1957

Twelve Step fellowship of men and women who share experiences, strength, and hope with each other to recover from compulsive gambling. Chapter development and monthly bulletins available for members.

Contact: P.O. Box 17173, Los Angeles, CA 90017. Call (213) 386-8789.

Inter-Congregational Alcoholism Program (ICAP)

- Founded 1979

Network of recovering alcoholic women in religious orders, specifically Roman Catholic women, who are or have been members of religious orders and who are in need of help due to alcoholism or chemical dependency. Information, referrals, phone support, assistance in meeting other members, and newsletters available.

Contact: 1515 N. Harlem Ave., #311, Oak Park, IL 60302. Call (708) 445-1400.

International Lawyers in Alcoholics Anonymous (ILAA)

- International
- Founded 1975

Twelve Step-focused clearinghouse for support groups for lawyers who are recovering alcoholics. Newsletters, annual conventions, and group development guidelines available upon request.

Contact: 14643 Sylvan St., Van Nuys, CA 91411.

International Nurses Anonymous

- International

Twelve Step fellowship of RNs, LPNs, and nursing students who are in recovery from chemical dependency, codependency, and/or other addiction-related problems.

Contact: Pat G., 1020 Sunset Dr., Lawrence, KS 66044. Call (913) 842-3893 or (913) 749-2626 (days).

International Pharmacists Anonymous

- National
- Founded 1987

Twelve Step groups of recovering pharmacists and pharmacy students recovering from any addiction. Newsletter, conferences, meetings, and networking available.

> **Contact:** Nan, 32 Cedar Grove Rd., Annandale, NJ 08801. Call (908) 730-9072 or (908) 735–2789.

Jewish Alcoholics, Chemically Dependent Persons and Significant Others (JACS)

- National
- Founded 1980

Twelve Step-oriented support groups for alcoholics and chemically dependent Jews, their families, and their community. Networking, Twelve Step work, retreats, literature, and help in starting local chapters available.

> **Contact:** 197 E. Broadway, New York, NY 10002. Call (212) 473-4747.

Nar-Anon, Inc.

- International
- Founded 1967

Worldwide organization offering self-help recovery to families and friends of addicts. This is the partner program to Narcotics Anonymous (NA). It is a Twelve Step-based program like Al-Anon, the partner fellowship to Alcoholics Anonymous (AA).

> **Contact:** Nar-Anon Family Group Headquarters, P.O. Box 2562, Palos Verdes, CA 90274-0119. Call (310) 547-5800.

Narcotics Anonymous (NA)

- International
- Founded 1953

Fellowship of men and women who have a drug problem. Recovering addicts meet regularly and fashion their program of recovery along the lines of AA's Twelve Steps. Founded by former AA members who were polyaddicted and wanted to shift focus from a specific type of drug (e.g., alcohol) to any and all mind-altering drugs, legal or not.

> **Contact:** P.O. Box 9999, Van Nuys, CA 91409. Call (818) 780-3951.

National Association for Native American Children of Alcoholics

- National
- Founded 1988

Support network for Native American children of alcoholics. Provides education, training, newsletter, and conferences.

> **Contact:** NANACOA, P.O. Box 18736, Seattle, WA 98118. Call (206) 322-5601.

National Association of Adult Children of Dysfunctional Families

- Regional
- Founded 1990

Aims to raise awareness regarding the issues of adult children of dysfunctional families. Facilitates networking of survivors and professionals alike to assist adult children in moving from victims to advocates through recovery.

> **Contact:** Amy D., NAACDF, P.O. Box 463, Fond du Lac, WI 54936-0463. Call (414) 921-6991.

Nicotine Anonymous World Services

- International
- Founded 1985

Self-help groups using the Twelve Step program for people who want to help themselves and others recover from nicotine addiction and live free of nicotine in all forms.

> **Contact:** 2118 Greenwich St., San Francisco, CA 94123. Call (415) 922-8575.

O-Anon

- International
- Founded 1975

Fellowship of friends and relatives of compulsive overeaters. Follows the Twelve Step program adapted from AA.

> **Contact:** P.O. Box 4305, San Pedro, CA 90731. Call (310) 547-1430.

Overcomers Outreach, Inc.

- International
- Founded 1985

Ministry of self-help groups for people who could benefit from a secular Twelve Step group in the Christian community. Includes alcoholics, drug addicts, compulsive eaters, gamblers, sexual addicts, codependents, etc. Newsletter, group development guidelines, and conferences available.

> **Contact:** 2290 W. Whittier Blvd., #A/D, La Habra, CA 90631. Call (310) 697-3994.

Overeaters Anonymous, Inc.

- International
- Founded 1960

Twelve Step fellowship of men and women who through shared experience, strength, and hope are working to solve their common problem—compulsive eating. Literature, magazine, worldwide meeting directory, newsletter.

> **Contact:** Overeaters Anonymous, Inc., P.O. Box 44020, Rio Rancho, NM 87174-4020. Call (505) 891-2664 or fax (505) 891-4320.

Oxford House, Inc.

Oxford Houses are houses that groups of recovering individuals, many of whom use Twelve Step-oriented programs (typically AA and NA) to stay clean and sober, rent to live together in an environment supportive of their recovery efforts. Each house is self-run and self-supported and follows a standardized system of democratic operation. For further information, see chapter 6.

> **Contact:** Oxford House, Inc., 9312 Colesville Road, Silver Spring, MD 20901. Call (301) 587-2916.

Pill Addicts Anonymous

- International
- Founded 1979

A Twelve Step-oriented fellowship for all who seek freedom from addiction to prescribed and over-the-counter mood-changing pills and drugs. Group members share their experience, strength, and hope to stay clean and help others to achieve sobriety.

> **Contact:** P.O. Box 278, Reading, PA 19603. Call (215) 372-1128.

Psychologists Helping Psychologists

- National
- Founded 1990

For doctoral-level psychologists or students who have had personal experience with alcohol or drugs. The aim is to support each other in recovery and to educate the psychology community. Regional and national get-togethers, newsletter.

Contact: 240 Waverly Place, #54, Waverly Place, New York, NY 10018.

Rational Recovery Systems (RR)

- International
- Founded 1986

Helps people recover from substance abuse and addictive behavior through self-reliance and self-help groups based on rational-emotive therapy techniques. It stresses secular-approach, nonspiritual self-help with groups run by "professional advisors"; short-term (six to nine months is typical). Group development guidelines, newsletter, and literature available.

Contact: P.O. Box 800, Lotus, CA 95651. Call (916) 621-4374.

Recovering Couples Anonymous (RCA)

- National
- Founded 1988

A Twelve Step group that helps couples restore intimacy, communication, and trust and learn healthier tools for maintaining these elements. Generally for couples involved in a committed relationship and in recovery from chemical dependency themselves.

Contact: P.O. Box 27617, Golden Valley, MN 55422. Call Deb M. (612) 473-3752.

S-Anon

- International
- Founded 1984

Twelve Step group for persons who have a friend or family member with a problem of sexual addiction. Assistance available for starting groups and conferences. Quarterly newsletter also available.

Contact: P.O. Box 5117, Sherman Oaks, CA 91413. Call (818) 990-6910.

Secular Organizations for Sobriety (Save Ourselves)

- International
- Founded 1986

Mutual help for alcoholics and addicts who want to acknowledge their disease and maintain sobriety as a separate issue from religion or spirituality.

Contact: P.O. Box 5, Buffalo, NY 14215. Call (716) 834-2922.

Sex Addicts Anonymous

- National
- Founded 1977

Twelve Step-oriented fellowship in which members share their experience, strength, and hope with one another to solve their common problem and gain freedom from compulsive sexual behavior.

Contact: P.O. Box 3038, Minneapolis, MN 55403. Call (612) 339-0217.

Sex and Love Addicts Anonymous

- International
- Founded 1989

Fellowship of relatives, friends, and significant others who share their experience and strength to find solutions to the problems of dealing with codependent sex and love addiction.

Contact: P.O. Box 614, Brookline, MA 02146-9998.

Sexaholics Anonymous

- International
- Founded 1979

Program of recovery for those who want help to stop sexually self-destructive thinking and behavior. Telephone network, quarterly newsletter, literature, and books available.

Contact: P.O. Box 300, Simi Valley, CA 93062. Call (818) 704-9854 or (805) 581-3343.

Sexual Compulsives Anonymous

- International
- Founded 1982

Men and women who share their experience, strength, and hope to solve their common problem and help others to recover from sexual compulsion. Twelve Step-oriented.

> **Contact:** P.O. Box 1585, New York, NY 10113-0935. Call (212) 439-1123 (NY); (312) 589-5856 (Chicago); or (213) 859-5585 (West Coast).

Social Workers Helping Social Workers

- National
- Founded 1980

An organization to promote recovery from chemical dependency among social workers and matriculating social work students.

> **Contact:** 25 South St., Goshen, CT 06756. Call (203) 489-3808.

Suggested Reading

Al-Anon Faces Alcoholism. New York: Al-Anon Family Group Headquarters, Inc., 1988.

Al-Anon's Twelve Steps and Twelve Traditions. New York: Al-Anon Family Group Headquarters, Inc., 1988.

Alcoholics Anonymous (The Big Book). New York: AA World Services, Inc., 1984.

Alcoholics Anonymous Comes of Age. New York: AA World Services, Inc., 1989.

Gorski, Terence T. *Relapse Prevention Therapy with Chemically Dependent Criminal Offenders: A Guide for Counselors, Therapists, and Criminal Justice Professionals.* Independence, Mo.: Herald House, 1994.

———. *Understanding the Twelve Steps: A Guide for Counselors, Therapists, and Recovering People.* New York: Prentice Hall Press, 1989.

Hope, Faith and Courage: Stories from the Fellowship of Cocaine Anonymous. Los Angeles: Cocaine Anonymous World Services, Inc., 1993.

It Works: How and Why: The Twelve Steps and Twelve Traditions of Narcotics Anonymous. Van Nuys, Calif.: World Service Office, Inc., 1993.

Milam, J. R., and K. Ketcham. *Under the Influence.* New York: Bantam Books, 1984.

Molloy, J. Paul. *Self-Run, Self-Supported Houses for More Effective Recovery from Alcohol and Drug Addiction.* US Dept. of Health and Human Services, Public Health Service (Rockville, Md.), DHHS Publication No. (SMA) 93-1678, 1993.

Narcotics Anonymous (The Blue Book). Van Nuys, Calif.: World Service Office, Inc., 1987.

Robertson, Nan. *Getting Better: Inside Alcoholics Anonymous.* New York: William Morrow and Company, Inc., 1988.

Rogers, Ron L., and Chandler S. McMillin. *Under Your Own Power: A Secular Approach to Twelve Step Programs*. New York: Putnam Publishing Group, 1993.

Twelve Steps and Twelve Traditions (The Twelve and Twelve). New York: AA World Services, Inc., 1984.

Further Resources Written or Co-Written by the Author . . .

Books:

Read, Edward M., and Dennis C. Daley. *Getting High and Doing Time: What's the Connection? A Recovery Guide for Alcoholics and Drug Addicts in Trouble with the Law*. Laurel, Md.: American Correctional Association, 1990.

————. *You've Got the Power: A Recovery Guide for Young People with Alcohol and Drug Problems*. Laurel, Md.: American Correctional Association, 1993.

Articles:

"A Conspiracy of Silence: Alcoholism and the Probation Officer." *Perspectives* [American Probation and Parole Association Magazine] (Winter 1989).

"Euphoria on the Rocks: Understanding Crack Addiction." *Federal Probation* (December 1992).

"Identifying the Alcoholic: A Practical Guide for the Probation Officer." *Federal Probation* 52 (September 1988).

"The Alcoholic, the Probation Officer, and AA: A Viable Team Approach to Supervision." *Federal Probation* (March 1987).

"Twelve Steps to Sobriety: Probation Officers Working the Program." *Federal Probation* 54 (December 1990).

"Walking the Talk":
A Glossary of "Program" Vernacular

ANNIVERSARY. Often used interchangeably with "birthday" to note someone's sobriety date, typically a specific day that marks the member's last drink or drug. Anniversary meetings are often celebratory in atmosphere and offer an important personal testimony to newcomers early in their program involvement; they can see it really does work as persons declare their anniversaries and get acknowledged for their respective periods of time clean or sober. Anniversaries are computed in increments of one year.

BIG BOOK. The colloquial term for the primary publication read by most recovering alcoholics, entitled *Alcoholics Anonymous*. It contains Bill Wilson's story, AA's theory on alcoholism, an introduction to the Twelve Steps, and many personal stories by AA pioneers.

BLUE BOOK. The colloquial term for the primary publication read by most recovering addicts, entitled *Narcotics Anonymous*.

BOTTOM. "Hitting bottom" is the customary phrase to describe the end moment of one's active addiction that resulted in a decision to make a change, to seek abstinence, or to ask for help. Everyone's bottom is different; for some it may result in homelessness, but for others it may stay restricted to inner turmoil, guilt, and pain with little or no outward signs of adverse consequences. Most program participants relate to some type of "bottom" in describing their decision (or coercion, in many cases) to seek help in a Twelve Step-oriented fellowship.

CHARACTER DEFECTS. The phrase used most frequently within the context of Step Four and having to do with the search for and acknowledgment of one's personality shortcomings that present a barrier to growth and recovery.

CHIP. A medallion given to participants of Twelve Step groups for various lengths of sobriety or abstinence.

CHIP MEETING. A Twelve Step group that takes a few minutes to acknowledge member anniversaries (see above), with medallions or "chips," usually during "half-time" but sometimes at the very beginning or very end. Often at the very end of the ceremony the leader will say, "Now for the most important person in the room, the person who has twenty-four hours' sober or clean time or simply desires a new way of life." The applause for this person will often outdo the applause for the person celebrating ten years!

CLEAN. Another term used by self-help group participants for staying abstinent; usually the one preferred by members of Narcotics Anonymous and Twelve Step programs other than Alcoholics Anonymous, where "sober" is the preferred term.

COMPLACENCY. Getting overconfident about one's recovery status. "Complacency" leads to fewer meetings, thinking one has it "together," and sloppy working of the Twelve Steps.

DOUBLE WINNER. Usually a term identifying a member of *both* AA and Al-Anon, or *both* NA and Nar-Anon.

DRY DRUNK. The phrase used to describe the alcoholic who is abstinent or "dry" but not working a program, not growing, and not adding anything to his or her life to replace the drug that has been removed. Being a "dry drunk" could also mean displaying the typical signs and attributes of active addiction despite the absence of alcohol: moodiness, emotional instability, irritability, free-floating anger, excessive criticism, and so on.

EASY DOES IT. A commonly used AA slogan suggesting that persons in recovery slow down and not fall prey to overdoing, overcontrolling, or overcompensating in areas of their lives now that active addiction is not the problem. It is cautioned: Take it one day at a time, stop and smell the roses, and avoid trying to suddenly, quickly, or obsessively manage the rest of one's life to compensate for "lost time."

ELEVENTH STEP. Often the full version of this Step is shortened to simply mean the amount of time and attention one might place on working toward a habit of regular meditation (or prayer, as the case may be) or a deepening sense of spirituality and connectedness to the world at large. Some meetings are called "Eleventh Step" meetings and focus exclusively on this aspect of one's recovery, the effort to move beyond the Self and into comfortable, spiritually based sobriety. For example, someone might say, "I do an Eleventh Step every morning; it's my way of starting the day by meditating and asking my Higher Power for guidance."

ENABLER. A person who unwittingly furthers or helps perpetuate someone's addiction by either action or inaction, resulting in a potentially devastating failure to intervene. The stereotypical nondrinking "co-alcoholic" spouse who covers for, rationalizes, and minimizes the addict's alcohol dependency is one example of an enabler.

FIRST THINGS FIRST. A slogan that emphasizes the importance a member must place on staying away from the first drink or drug, since it is the "first one that will get you drunk." A less literal translation spills over into the area of sober living and how important it is to stay in the moment and not needlessly project oneself into the future. By staying focused on the "next right thing" (to do, to say, to think), one is less likely to get distracted by negative thoughts, emotions, or obsessions.

FRIEND OF BILL'S. A member of AA, as in a "friend of Bill" Wilson, AA's co-founder. Sometimes seen on bumper stickers, sometimes used in casual conversation between people to determine whether or not the other is in the Fellowship.

G.O.D. Often used as an acronym for "Group of Drunks." Old-timers will suggest that those reluctant to embrace the word *GOD* might pause and think of making their Higher Power the actual group or meeting they attend—their Higher Power can be anything but themselves!

H.A.L.T. This is a commonly used acronym for Hungry, Angry, Lonely, or Tired: four conditions or states of mind the recovering person, especially the newcomer, needs to stay mindful of in terms of avoiding relapse (to the drug of choice or to the less productive and dangerous thinking or behavior patterns that might eventually lead to relapse). The less hungry, angry, lonely, or tired a person is, the greater the chance of remaining sober, in the fullest sense of the word.

HIGHER POWER. Sometimes shortened to HP, the phrase is often used by program members reluctant or uncomfortable with the word *God*. It appears in the Second Step, "Came to believe that a Power greater than ourselves could restore us to sanity." It is fairly typical for someone to qualify his or her use of the term *God* for newcomers so as not to offend or sound religious by saying the following: "My Higher Power, whom I now choose to call God . . ." The term is rooted in the notion that most persons cannot recover from addiction all alone; they must reach a level of acceptance that renders them willing to accept help outside of themselves, even if for the confirmed atheist it simply means the group itself.

HOME GROUP. To be in a Twelve Step fellowship and have a home group (something all newcomers should be encouraged to acquire) means that there is one particular meeting a person returns to week after week, getting to know others and becoming a real part of the informal "family" system. Such a person's absence is usually conspicuous and may in fact result in inquiring telephone calls. By habitually attending one particular meeting, the newcomer sees others get better over time and invites much more personal attention that he or she may otherwise shy away from.

INVENTORY. Mentioned in the Fourth Step and used in the phrase "taking inventory," this means examining oneself or others in the context of the Fourth or Tenth Step; for example, "After taking inventory of myself I came to see the part I really play in damaging the relationship I have with my spouse." Someone who honestly takes inventory, oftentimes with the help of a sponsor, is moving toward true sobriety where personal morality and a newfound sense of right and wrong are constantly examined.

KEEP COMING BACK. The frequently used phrase to encourage newcomers to return to the group or meeting, urging them to make meetings a real part of their life. Old-timers use it half-jokingly to remind themselves of their continuing need to stay close to the program for help and guidance in other areas of their life long after the abstinence part may have been mastered.

KEEP IT SIMPLE. A slogan designed to remind program participants not to complicate their lives, not to get lost in misplaced priorities and distractions. The important point is "not to drink, get to meetings, and say your prayers"; nothing more, nothing less. It has been said that the Twelve Steps are a "simple program for complicated people." Use of this slogan, often followed by the phrase "and do the next right thing," guides many program participants through emotionally trying times.

LETTING GO. Often expressed as "Let go and let God," the idea is to remind recovering people of the peacefulness and serenity possible if they earnestly work the Third Step ("Made a decision to turn our will and our lives over to the care of God *as we understood Him*") and make an effort not to control every aspect of their life. The message is clear: Stop trying to manipulate, run, or control everything. Let go and let the process take care of itself.

LIVE AND LET LIVE. This slogan reminds people in recovery programs to stay focused on themselves, on "doing the next right thing," as it is sometimes said, and on not getting caught up in or distracted by what others do with themselves or their lives.

MARATHON MEETING. Usually held over the holidays or other special times. Groups will hold meetings around the clock.

MEETINGS AFTER THE MEETINGS. These are the small informal gatherings of program participants after the regular meeting that take place anywhere from local coffee shops to people's homes. By choosing to socialize afterwards, members deepen their recovery network and develop friendships with others similarly bent on staying clean and sober.

NETWORK. A term used most frequently by NA members to refer to their circle of friends within the program. The wider people's networks are, the greater likelihood they will not find themselves around negative peer influences that typically precede relapse.

NEWCOMER. Someone new to the Fellowship, usually within the first few months of his or her recovery experience.

NINETY IN NINETY (90 IN 90). Most veteran Twelve Step-goers will strongly encourage newcomers to introduce themselves to the recovery process and meetings in general by committing themselves to attending "ninety meetings in ninety days." By so doing, addicts not only reduce the chances of relapse (after all, they may have been using every day and now are attending a meeting every day in place of their using), but it also opens the door to their overall exposure to the Fellowship, including a variety of different meetings.

OLD-TIMER. Primarily a term to describe the AA member who has been around the program a long time, typically someone who has twenty years or more of continuous sobriety.

ONE DAY AT A TIME. Probably the best-known slogan of all. It means what it says: "Don't think about staying sober or clean for the rest of your life. . . . Concentrate on taking it *one day at a time.*" Program old-timers postulate that even the worst of the worst (in terms of addiction severity) can remain straight for twenty-four hours, even if it means breaking it down incrementally to hours or minutes. By thinking it through (perhaps focusing on one's last drunk or drugging experience), saying the Serenity prayer, and getting to a meeting "one day at a time," the newcomer is able to work through the initial cravings and make it to the next day, when the process may have to start all over again. People who have been around a while also take advantage of this slogan just in terms of coping with life's demands in general.

PEOPLE, PLACES, AND THINGS. The phrase customarily used to remind Twelve Step participants that not only are they ultimately powerless over their drug of choice (i.e., if it is ingested), but they are also unable to completely control "people, places, and things." To keep this in mind as part of their program they must stay focused on sobriety, staying clean and sober "one day at a time," and not being overly influenced by worldly matters. A person, a place, or a thing must not become an excuse to use or drink. "Turning it over" (see below) to one's Higher Power (HP) is just as important as acknowledging powerlessness over the actual drug.

PIGEON. Primarily an AA term for a sponsor's "sponsee"; seems to be a word on its way out; used primarily by old-timers.

PROMISES, THE. Referred to as "the Promises," this phrase refers to a paragraph within the book *Alcoholics Anonymous* (the "Big Book"), on pages 83–84, that assures its readers of the various guarantees associated with continued sobriety. See pages 74–75 of this book for a complete quote.

RELAPSE. The process as well as specific behavior involving a return of addictive disease symptoms, such as drinking alcohol and/or using drugs after a period of abstinence. A full relapse (vs. a "lapse") usually connotes a serious breakdown of one's recovery plan. Relapse is often preceded by individually specific warning signs (cognitive, emotional, and spiritual) *before* the actual drink or drug is consumed.

SELF-CENTERED FEAR. The fear of losing something you have or not getting something you demand.

SERENITY PRAYER. "God grant me the serenity to accept the things I cannot change, the courage to change the things I can, and the wisdom to know the difference." This is the prayer that over the years has become very much a part of the Twelve Step community. Most program members serious about their recovery can easily recite the Serenity Prayer and do so frequently throughout the day.

SERVICE WORK. Getting involved in "service work" inevitably signifies a little extra commitment and time on the part of a Fellowship participant. It means volunteering to be chairperson, working the telephone desk, being secretary or treasurer for a group, bringing meetings to area hospitals and institutions (H and I Committee work), or even making coffee for a particular group.

SEVENTH STEP PRAYER. Taken from page 76 of the Big Book, this is a prayer learned and recited by many people within the Twelve Step fellowships. It is so named because it capsulizes what the Seventh Step suggests when one "humbly ask[s] Him to remove our shortcomings." It goes like this: "My Creator, I am now willing that you should have all of me, good and bad. I pray that you now remove from me every single defect of character which stands in the way of my usefulness to you and my fellows. Grant me strength, as I go out from here, to do your bidding. Amen."

SLIP. Primarily an AA term meaning that someone has relapsed, returned to active addiction, or simply had a drink (or drug) consequently breaking his or her period of abstinence.

SOBER. Used widely in AA circles to denote abstinence from alcohol and other mood-altering drugs. "Sober" is to AA what "clean" is to NA. Most program members acknowledge the broader context of this word and use it accordingly. To be sober means to live a physically, emotionally, and spiritually balanced lifestyle. Excessive demands and extremism are common among addicted persons in recovery; by living sober the addict or alcoholic focuses on tempering these "character defects" that surface despite abstinence.

SPIN-DRYER. An AA term, used typically by persons who recovered on their own within the "rooms" of AA, to describe the twenty-eight-day inpatient rehabilitation programs that began to flourish (and still do in many parts of the country) during the 1980s as a direct response to the growth of the "treatment industry." Obviously, the term is often used derisively.

SPONSEE. Someone who is sponsored by someone else; the original term, started early in AA, was *pigeon* (see above), but it seems to be on the way out.

SPONSOR. Someone within a Twelve Step fellowship who has experience in the program, usually in excess of a year of continuous clean and sober time, and who is willing to mentor and guide a newcomer. Anyone serious about working the Twelve Step program is strongly encouraged to find someone, preferably of the same sex, to sponsor him or her. See pages 112–119 for further information on sponsorship.

STEP-SPONSOR. A sponsor used primarily for the interpretation and application of the Twelve Steps in a person's recovery.

STEPS. The Twelve Steps as originally conceived by AA and used by any number of different self-help groups.

STINKING THINKING. The term used to describe the negative thoughts, emotions, or feelings that might precede an actual relapse or just a return to uncomfortable living within sobriety. For example, people who are forever "comparing their insides to other people's outsides" are exhibiting stinking thinking at its best.

TEMPORARY SPONSOR. Newcomers are encouraged to ask someone to be their "temporary sponsor" as soon as possible, ostensibly while they are looking for a permanent one. It is a good way to get someone moving in the direction of sponsorship.

TENTH STEP. Doing a Tenth Step means continuing to pay attention, on a daily basis, to one's relationship to the world and honestly accepting responsibility when things go wrong (and right, like not taking a drink or a drug that day!). Some program participants do a Tenth Step every night before bed; others do "on-the-spot" checks. For example, a person might say in a meeting, "I did a serious Tenth Step yesterday after an argument with my boss; I was wrong and had to come clean about it and apologize."

THINK, THINK, THINK. This slogan suggests the program participant "think the drink or drug through," that is, reflect on what it will really mean *in the end* if one makes the ill-fated decision to take that first drink or drug. In AA it is often said that it's the "first drink that gets you drunk." The first one ignites the engines of compulsion and loss of control, not the second or third. By thinking through the whole scenario, ugly consequences included, one buys the time necessary to make a phone call, get to a meeting, or simply make a better decision not to use or drink.

THIRD STEP PRAYER. Taken from page 63 of the Big Book, this is a prayer learned and recited by many people within the Twelve Step fellowships as they "work" the Third Step, "Made a decision to turn our will and our lives over to the care of God *as we understood Him.*" It goes like this: "God, I offer myself to Thee—to build with me and to do with me as Thou wilt. Relieve me of the bondage of self, that I may better do Thy will. Take away my difficulties, that victory over them may bear witness to those I would help of Thy Power, Thy Love, and Thy Way of life. May I do Thy will always!"

THIRTEENTH STEPPING. A phrase used to describe people, usually men early in recovery, who take advantage of women early in recovery by focusing on dating and intimate encounters, not true Twelfth Step work.

THREE CS. An Al-Anon term for the following reminder: "I didn't Cause it (i.e., the alcoholism or drug abuse); I can't Control it; and I can't Cure it." Newcomers to Al-Anon often feel exactly the opposite; this helpful message drives the point home during times of pain or confusion about their loved one in trouble with alcohol or drugs.

TURN IT OVER. This means having faith that a Higher Power will take care of whatever is troubling you. Twelve Step participants believe that as long as they stay clean and sober, the details of life will be very safely handled by HP. It does not mean relinquishing free choice or the exercise of individual freedom.

TWELFTH-STEPPING. To "twelfth-step" someone or to be doing Twelfth Step work simply means carrying the message, trying to help another addict or alcoholic achieve sobriety. It can have many different variations or components, depending upon the member's interests and/or skills. A person may do service work, answer calls from the AA or NA "desk" to take someone to his or her first meeting (or even to the hospital, in some cases), or simply sponsor someone. All are aspects of Twelve Step work.

TWELVE AND TWELVE. The colloquial term for the second most widely read book by recovering alcoholics, entitled *Twelve Steps and Twelve Traditions*. This book outlines each Step and Tradition, discussing practical applications and associated philosophy. NA just recently published its version of this material, entitled *It Works: How and Why.*

TWO-STEPPER. Someone who works the First and the Twelfth Steps skipping the ten Steps in between and consequently lacking sufficient depth to his or her sobriety. A two-stepper typically maintains abstinence but avoids work on personal growth (Steps Two through Eleven) and instead focuses only on trying to recruit or sponsor newer members (Step Twelve), often to his or her own detriment as well as that of potential followers.

UNMANAGEABILITY. The term frequently used to talk about the second part of Step One (". . . that our lives had become unmanageable"). Active addiction leads to unmanageability; so does abstinence without change or "recovery." AAs and other Twelve Step program members strongly believe that their addiction is physical, mental, and emotional; and that unless they concentrate on all three aspects, their lives can become just as unmanageable, regardless of whether or not they are actually "practicing" (using).

USING. Or "practicing" one's addiction. Usually connotes drugs other than alcohol. AAs typically refer to their use as "drinking"; members of NA typically refer to their active addiction as "using."

WORKING THE PROGRAM/STEPS. This means living a life of recovery based upon the Twelve Steps. People who work the program in this way will remain abstinent, go to meetings, read literature, talk and meet with a sponsor, and generally try to incorporate the "program" into their life.

Accountability, 25–26, 33–35, 38–39, 149–53

Addicted offenders, 2–6, 12–13
    family system, 126–42
    meetings, 81–89
    recovery, 63–79, 150–52
    referrals, 89–95
    resistance, 99–107
    supervision techniques, 81–123

Addiction, 1–4, 12–13, 149
    assessment, 35–38
    disease vs. willful misconduct, 32–35
    effect on family, 126–42
    recovery process, 63–79, 150–52

Al-Anon, 126–39, 151, 157

Alcohol drinking, 28–35
    societal costs, 29

Alcoholics Anonymous (AA), 6, 38–40, 157
    beginnings of, 41–43
    differences from NA, 95–97
    misconceptions about, 57–59
    referrals to, 7–8, 81, 89–95, 120, 151

Twelve Step literacy, 7–9, 61–79
Twelve Traditions, 44–55

Alcoholism, 31–35

American Medical Association, 43

Americans with Disabilities Act, 43

Antisocial personality disorder, 27–28

Assessment, 35–40, 90–92, 152–53

Attitudes, 11–40

C.A.G.E. Questionnaire, 36–38

Cocaine Anonymous (CA), 93–94, 160

Community corrections system
    companion resources, 125–48
    mission statement, 2, 149
    referrals for addicted offenders, 89–95, 151
    supervision techniques, 81–123

Community resources, 125–48, 151

Confrontation, 38–39

Court-mandated referrals, 108–12

Court slips, 108–9

Denial, 22, 99–107

Disease vs. willful misconduct, 32–35

Emotional disorder, coexisting with
    chemical dependency, 27–28

Empathy, 152–53

Enabling, 25–26, 128

Family system, 125–42

Foundation Steps (1–3), 63–66

Gamblers Anonymous (GA), 6, 163

"Higher Power," 64–65, 72, 76–77,
    97–99, 100–1, 138–39

Honesty, 13–14

Interventions, 22, 38–39

Lying, 20–21

Maintenance Steps (10–12), 75–79

Meeting attendance, 81–89, 99–107

Mental illness, coexisting with
    chemical dependency, 27–28

Misconceptions
    about AA, 57–59
    about Al-Anon, 132–34

Moral weakness, 23–24

Motivation, 38–40

Mutual support groups, 155–69

Nar-Anon, 126–27, 139–40, 151, 164

Narcotics Anonymous (NA), 6, 55–57,
    95–97, 164

Nonbelievers, program options, 97–99

Open-mindedness, 14

Oxford House, 144–48, 151, 166

Positive authority, 38–40

Postresidential treatment, 142–48

Rational Recovery (RR), 98, 121, 167

Reconciliation (Steps 7–9), 72–75, 139

Recovery, 63–79, 150–52
    role of family, 125–42

Referrals, 89–95, 120, 151

Reflection (Steps 4–6), 67–72

Relapse, 22–23, 126, 142–48

Resistance, 99–107, 120, 151

Respect, 21, 153

Rules of engagement, 128–32

Screening tools, 36–38

Self-righteous indignation (SRI),
    15–26, 150

Serenity Prayer, 104

Smith, Dr. Bob, 42, 53, 114

Spirituality, 64–66, 72, 76–78, 97–99, 100–1, 133

Sponsorship, 111–19

Substance abuse
    addicted offenders, 2–6, 12–13
    effect on family, 126–42
    societal costs, 29
    statistics about, 1–2

Supervision accountability, 149–53

Supervision, community, 81–23
    assessment, 90–92
    do's and don'ts, 120–23
    meeting attendance, 81–89, 99–107
    newcomer offenders, 115–17
    referrals, 89–95
    resistance, 99–107
    slip-signing scams, 108–12
    sponsorship, 112–15, 118–19

Support groups (self-help), 155–69

Treatment, 38–40, 150–52
    industry, 43
    role of family, 125–42

Trust, 21, 81, 153

Twelve Steps, 6, 61–79, 86, 120–23, 133, 137–39, 150–52

Twelve Traditions, 44–55, 84, 133

Willingness, 14, 71

Willpower, 64

Wilson, William Griffith ("Bill"), 41–42, 53, 114

About the author

Ed Read, LCSW, NCAC II, is a U.S. Probation Officer for the District of Columbia in Washington, D.C., and has worked in the field of corrections for over fifteen years. He is a graduate of Columbia University School of Social Work with prior experience in the federal prison system, county probation and parole, and with the Administrative Office of the U.S. Courts (Probation Division) as a drug program and policy specialist.

He is currently a line supervision officer within a specialized chemical dependency unit for the U.S. Probation Office and has written extensively in the area of addictions for a variety of professional trade publications, including two co-authored ACA books targeted directly to the addicted offender. Mr. Read also is a Federal Judicial Center faculty member and serves as both a new officer instructor and consultant.

Other titles of interest . . .

Getting Started in AA
by Hamilton B.

This easy-to-comprehend handbook contains practical suggestions for staying sober; summaries of how to use the AA fellowship principles, concepts, and slogans; information about meetings and groups; descriptions of how the fellowship is organized and its functions; selections of historical references and anecdotes; and glossaries. Softcover, 160 pp.

Order No. 1308

Men in Recovery
Finding Our Direction
by Merle Fossum

Drawing on the lessons of AA, Al-Anon, and the Twelve Step recovery model, the author brings to light what has been learned about recovering men and the special problems they face. Fossum's innovative application of the Twelve Step process to men's issues can help all men become whole, healthy human beings. Softcover, 193.

Order No. 5041

Free at Last
Daily Meditations by and for Inmates

For inmates who have escaped the prison of chemical dependency and those who are still bound by addiction, the beauty of these meditations lies in the voice of the many writers—a voice that is at once hopeful, sad, brave, and determined. Whether for daily inspiration or used as a springboard for meeting discussions, the stories found in this book are filled with wisdom and understanding. Softcover, 375 pp.

Order No. 7807
